Ninja Dual Air Fryer Cookbook UK

Effortless & Delicious Air Fryer Recipes with Pictures for Beginners and Family | 2000+ Days Crisp-Enjoyment for an Easier and Healthier Lifestyle | Full-color Edition

Evie Reynolds

© Copyright 2023-All Rights Reserved.

This document is geared towards providing exact and reliable information concerning the topic and issue covered. The publication is sold with the idea that the publisher is not required to render accounting, officially permitted, or otherwise, qualified services. If advice is necessary, legal or professional, a practiced individual in the profession should be ordered.

In no way is it legal to reproduce, duplicate, or transmit any part of this document in either electronic means or in printed format. Recording of this publication is strictly prohibited, and any storage of this document is not allowed unless with written permission from the publisher. All rights reserved.

The information provided herein is stated to be truthful and consistent, in that any liability, in terms of inattention or otherwise, by any usage or abuse of any policies, processes, or Instructions: contained within is the solitary and utter responsibility of the recipient reader. Under no circumstances will any legal responsibility or blame be held against the publisher for any reparation, damages, or monetary loss due to the information herein, either directly or indirectly.

Respective authors own all copyrights not held by the publisher.

The information herein is offered for informational purposes solely and is universal as such. The presentation of the information is without a contract or any type of guarantee assurance.

The trademarks that are used are without any consent, and the publication of the trademark is without permission or backing by the trademark owner. All trademarks and brands within this book are for clarifying purposes only, are owned by the owners themselves, and are not affiliated with this document.

Contents

Introduction

Fundamentals of Ninja Foodi Dual Air Fryer

4-Week Diet Plan

Chapter 1 Breakfast Recipes

Quick Hard Boiled Eggs /8
Classic Egg in a Hole /8
Cinnamon Banana Bread with Walnuts /9
Easy Baked Bagels /9
Vanilla Butter Toast /10
Fried Apples with Cinnamon Oats /10
Traditional Avocado Egg Cups /11
Lemony Salmon Quiche /11
Homemade Sesame Yogurt Bagels /12
Sweet French Toasts /12

Chapter 2 Snacks and Starter Recipes

Crispy Spicy Pumpkin Fries /13
Simple Potato Chips /13
Crispy Lemony Calamari Rings /14
Rosemary Cheese Turkey Croquettes /14
Crispy Breaded Mozzarella Sticks /15
Classic Soft Pretzels /15
Delicious Cheese Beef Taquitos /16
Fresh Crispy Fried Okra /16
Homemade Potato Waffle Fries /17
Crunchy Onion Rings /17
Salty Fresh Kale Chips /18
Cumin Cauliflower Poppers /18
Crispy Breaded Avocado Fries /19
Easy Potato Fries /19
Cheese Jalapeño Poppers with Spring Onion /20

Chapter 3 — Vegetables and Sides Recipes

Sweet Buttery Squash slices /21
Parmesan Asparagus /21
Quick Balsamic Asparagus /22
Spicy Crispy Green Tomatoes /22
Salty Garlicky Mushrooms /23
Refreshing Balsamic Brussel Sprouts /23
Chili Butternut Squash Cubes /24
Cheesy Garlic Broccoli /24
Spicy Spiced Butter Courgettes /25
Savoury Fried Rice with Peas & Carrots /25
Healthy Black Beans & Veggie Burgers /26
Sticky Tofu in Ginger Orange Sauce /26
Honey Glazed Carrots with Thyme /27
Traditional Hasselback Potatoes /27

Chapter 4 — Fish and Seafood Recipes

Cheese Prawn Salad with Cherry Tomatoes /28
Garlicky Teriyaki Wild Salmon /28
Cheese-Crusted Tuna Patties with Parsley /29
Garlicky Fried Salmon Fillets /29
Crispy Salmon Cakes with Mayonnaise /30
Nutritious Honey Glazed Tuna Steaks /30
Delicious Cod Cakes with Coriander /31
Buttery Fried Salmon Fillets /31
Tasty Lemony Salmon Fillets /32
Sweet and Spicy Salmon with Sesame /32
Healthy Fried Salmon with Asparagus /33
Homemade Breaded Tilapia Fillets /33
Crispy Cajun Cod Fillets /34
Fresh Garlic Butter Prawns with Parsley /34
Air Fried Salmon Fillets /35
Lemon-Chili Salmon /35
Tasty Sweet & Sour Salmon /36
Lemony Herbed Salmon with Asparagus /36

Chapter 5: Poultry Mains Recipes

Garlicky Cumin Chicken Thighs /37
Crunchy Breaded Chicken Breasts /37
Crispy Cheese Chicken Tenderloins /38
Baked Turkey Breast /38
Air Fryer Spiced Duck Legs /39
Beer-Marinated Duck Breast /39
Crispy Chicken Tenders /40
Crunchy Breaded Chicken Cutlets /40
Buttery Chicken Breast /41
Spicy Chicken Wings /41
Almond Crusted Chicken /42
Sweet Potato Chips-Crusted Chicken /42
Crispy Herbed Chicken /43
Buttery Bagel Crusted Chicken Strips /43
Lemony Cheese Chicken Breast /44
Hot and Spicy Chicken Breasts /44
Herbed Spicy Whole Chicken /45
Sour & Spicy Chicken Legs /45
Crispy Paprika Chicken Legs /46
Gingered Chicken Drumsticks /46
Honey & Mustard Chicken Drumsticks /47
Parmesan Chicken Breasts /47
Easy Baked Turkey Breast /48
Cheese & Spinach Stuffed Chicken Breasts /48

Chapter 6: Beef, Pork & Lamb Recipes

Easy Air Fried Lamb Steak /49
Tasty Beef Roast /49
BBQ Honey Pork Ribs /50
Simple Air Fried New York Strip Steak /50
Air Fryer Bacon Wrapped Hot Dogs /51
Herbed Garlic Pork Chops /51
Aromatic Cinnamon Lamb Meatballs /52
Chili-Garlic Lamb Loin Chops /52
Cajun Flank Steak /53
Herbed Garlic Lamb Chops /53
Baked Lamb Steaks /54
Herbed Beef Roast with Onion /54
Homemade BBQ Baby Back Ribs /55
Herbs Baked Pork Chops /55
Delicious Bacon Wrapped Pork Tenderloin /56
Simple Taco Seasoned Lamb Chops /56
Rosemary Garlic Lamb Chops /57
Easy Beef Sirloin Roast /57

Chapter 7 Dessert Recipes

Easy Butter Cake /58
Apple Crumble /58
Raisins & Walnuts Semolina Cake /59
Lemon Cheesecake /59
Vanilla Chocolate Cake /60
Butter Oats Cookies /60
Best Churros /61
Butter Brownies /61
Lime Mousse /62
Chocolate Pistachios Muffins /62
Chocolate Chip Mug Cakes /63
Cherry Crumble /63

Conclusion
Appendix 1 Measurement Conversion Chart
Appendix 2 Recipes Index

Introduction

Technological advancement has altered the way we live our daily lives in numerous ways, including how we cook food. The increasing awareness around eating healthier, trying to attain "body goals", and losing weight, without having to compromise on taste or giving up on our favorite foods has given rise to several innovative culinary technologies. A game changer within this realm is the Ninja Foodi Dual Air Fryer. Not only does this one kitchen appliance do all the cooking for you while requiring less attention, it saves significant time through its groundbreaking functions.

The Ninja Foodi Dual Air Fryer, as the name indicates, offers multi-cooking capabilities. This means that you can cook two dishes at once, not only saving time, and effort, but also ensuring your whole meal gets ready at the same time. Wish to prepare your main course with sides? The Ninja Foodi Dual lets you do it with ease. What's even better is that with the dual cooking option, you can very easily cook a big batch of a dish in one go, co-ordinating the cooking time to ensure nothing gets over or under– done. This air fryer also comes with a wonderful cookbook with delectable recipes perfect for gatherings and various occasions.

Fundamentals of Ninja Foodi Dual Air Fryer

What is Ninja Foodi Dual Air Fryer?

With its capacity to completely transform preparing meals, the Ninja Foodi Dual Air Fryer is a multifunctional cooking appliance which has become extremely well-liked among foodies. This air fryer provides a variety of cooking alternatives in a small appliance by fusing the advantages of a conventional air fryer alongside the ease of a multi-cooker.

Essentially, the Ninja Foodi Dual Air Fryer uses the force of rapid air innovation to produce crisp, golden outcomes with a lot less oil compared to conventional frying techniques. Through the use of technology, the dish is heated throughout, resulting in uniform cooking and a delicious crispness minus the need of excessive fat. Using the air fryer feature, you can make tasty and more nutritious versions of your favorite deep-fried foods like French fries, chicken wings, and even veggies.

The dual-zone functionality of the device is precisely what makes it unique. The appliance, which differs from conventional air fryers in that it has two distinct cooking zones, enables you to prepare two distinct foods at the same time at various temperatures and durations. This allows you to cook a main meal and a side dish at the same time, sparing you time and energy.

Additionally, the Ninja Foodi Dual Air Fryer is more capable than just air frying. It also offers choices for roasting, baking, air frying, and dehydrating, serving as a flexible multi-cooker. Users get the freedom to get creative with a variety of dishes, from delicious roast chicken to handmade pizzas and dried goods, with the programmable time and heat parameters.

The appliance's intuitive interface ranks as one of its most outstanding qualities. It makes cooking straightforward and accessible even to people with no prior cooking expertise due to its easy controls and crystal-clear digital display. Making the best use of the Ninja Foodie from the very beginning is ensured by the cookbook that comes with the appliance. It offers ideas for a variety of foods.

The nonstick coatings and washable parts of the gadget make cleaning quick and easy. For busy people and families, the practical component contributes to it being an appealing option.

Benefits of Using It

The Ninja Foodi Dual is an invaluable asset to every household owing to its numerous advantages. In this section we explore the benefits of utilizing this adaptable equipment:

- **Healthier Food:** Among the main advantages of this air fryer is its utilization of minimal oil when cooking. The Rapid Air Technique uses heated air to flow around the meal, giving it a crusty quality without using a lot of oil. This allows you to indulge in your favorite fried dishes while developing healthy eating practices.
- **Effective Usage:** The Ninja Foodi Dual's dual-zone functionality enables consumers to prepare two distinct meals at the same time while implementing different cooking settings. This preserves electricity in addition to saving time. It speeds dinner preparation, making it ideal for households and people with hectic schedules.
- **Cooking Flexibility:** In addition to air frying, this device is a multi-cooker. It may be used to make a variety of foods, from savory barbecues to flawlessly baked sweets. Due to its adaptability, you won't need as many home appliances, clearing up space in the kitchen and making cooking easier.
- **Simple to Use:** The Ninja Foodi Dual was created with ease of usage in consideration. Choosing cooking modes, temperatures, and times is simple because of the command panel's logical controls and bright LCD screen. This device is simple to use and yields precise outcomes whether the user is an experienced chef or an inexperienced one.
- **Consistent Cooking:** This air fryer guarantees consistent cooking due to its cutting-edge airflow innovation. There aren't any concentrated hot areas or cooking inconsistencies. Irrespective of the chosen cooking mode, users can depend on reliable results each time.
- **Space-Saving Structure:** The Ninja Foodi Dual has a petite structure that doesn't need much counter space, regardless of its outstanding array of capabilities. It is an attractive improvement for any home because of its minimalist style, which blends well with the majority of kitchen design elements.
- **Custom Cooking:** Cooking may be customized for every cooking zone using the gadget's temperature and timing controls. Even if you're seeking different textures in every dish, this degree of oversight guarantees that the food items come out just how you want them to.
- **Cost Reductions:** The Ninja Foodi Dual Air Fryer may conserve money over time by removing the requirement of several cooking devices. It is a comprehensive appliance which takes the place of conventional ovens, deep-frying pans, and more, minimizing the demand for extra kitchen appliances.

Different Modes of Ninja Dual Air Fryer

Function Buttons

Air Fry
1. Set crisper plate in place.
2. Add ingredients to the drawer and insert in your main unit.
3. Zone 1 is always the default. Select AIR FRY.
4. Adjust temperature and time accordingly using the TEMP and TIME arrows.
5. Press START/PAUSE to initiate the cooking process. You are free to remove the drawer and toss ingredients as cooking continues to ensure you attain even crisping.
6. Once cooking is complete, you will hear a beep sound, and 'End' shows on the display.
7. Use tongs to take out your food and your utensils.

Roast
1. Set crisper plate in place.
2. Add ingredients to the drawer and insert in your main unit.
3. Zone 1 is always the default. Select ROAST

4. Adjust temperature and time accordingly using the TEMP and TIME arrows.
5. Press START/PAUSE to initiate the cooking process.
6. Once cooking is complete, you will hear a beep sound, and 'End' shows on the display.
7. Use tongs to take out your food and your utensils.

Reheat
1. Set crisper plate in place.
2. Add ingredients to the drawer and insert in your main unit.
3. Zone 1 is always the default. Select REHEAT
4. Adjust temperature and time accordingly using the TEMP and TIME arrows.
5. Press START/PAUSE to initiate the cooking process.
6. Once cooking is complete, you will hear a beep sound, and 'End' shows on the display.
7. Use tongs to take out your food and your utensils.

Dehydrate
1. Set crisper plate in place.
2. Add ingredients to the drawer and insert in your main unit.
3. Zone 1 is always the default. Select DEHYDRATE.
4. Adjust temperature and time accordingly using the TEMP and TIME arrows.
5. Press START/PAUSE to initiate the dehydrating process.
6. Once cooking is complete, you will hear a beep sound, and 'End' shows on the display.
7. Use tongs to take out your food and your utensils.

Bake
1. Set crisper plate in place.
2. Add ingredients to the drawer and insert in your main unit.
3. Zone 1 is always the default. Select BAKE
4. Adjust temperature and time accordingly using the TEMP and TIME arrows.
5. Press START/PAUSE to initiate the cooking process.
6. Once cooking is complete, you will hear a beep sound, and 'End' shows on the display.
7. Use tongs to take out your food and your utensils.

Air Broil
1. Set crisper plate in place.
2. Add ingredients to the basket. Insert in your main unit.
3. Zone 1 is always the default. Select the AIR BROIL function.
4. Adjust temperature and time accordingly using the TEMP and TIME arrows.
5. Press START/PAUSE to initiate the process.
6. Once cooking is complete, you will hear a beep sound, and 'End' shows on the display.
7. Use tongs to take out your food and your utensils.
8. Slice and enjoy.

Operating Buttons
TEMP arrows: Use the up and down arrows to adjust the cook temperature before or during cooking.

TIME arrows: Use the up and down arrows to adjust the cook time in any function before or during the cook cycle.
SMART FINISH button: Automatically syncs the cook times to ensure both zones finish at the same time, even if there are different cook times.
MATCH COOK button: Automatically matches zone 2 settings to those of zone 1 to cook a larger amount of the same food, or cook different foods using the same function, temperature, and time.
START/PAUSE button: After selecting temperature and time, start cooking by pressing the START/PAUSE button. To pause cooking, first select the zone you would like to pause, then press the START/PAUSE button.
POWER BUTTON: The button turns the unit on and off and stops all cooking functions. **Standby Mode:** After 10 minutes of no interaction with the control panel, the unit will enter standby mode. The Power button will be dimly lit.
Hold Mode: Hold will appear on the unit while in SMART FINISH mode. One zone will be cooking, while the other zone will be holding until the times sync together.

Step-By-Step Using It

Using the Ninja Foodi Dual Air Fryer is a simple task for anyone. We are going to coach you through the fundamental operation of this adaptable device in this step-by-step manual.

Step 1: Preparation and Unpacking
Unpack the Ninja Foodi Dual Air Fryer and thoroughly examine every part before using it. Verify that all components are present and in excellent working order. Cooking baskets, crisper platters, and any other extras provided with the model you own must have been included with the primary machine.
Ensure that the device is placed on an uncluttered, level platform with ample ventilation, and provide sufficient room around it for appropriate airflow while cooking.

Step 2: Preheat your air fryer
It is important to get the equipment warmed up before you start cooking. The best outcomes are made possible by preheating the food. Following these procedures will pre-heat the air fryer properly:
Utilizing the power switch, turn on your Ninja Foodi Dual Air Fryer after plugging it in.
Pushing the appropriate switch on the control screen will let you choose the required cooking mode.
For warmup settings, adjust the temperatures and duration settings. Generally, you may pre-heat for a short period of time (usually 3-5 mins) at the precise heat that you intend to begin cooking at.
Click the "Start" toggle when you have chosen the warmup options. On the electronic display, a countdown clock appears as the gadget starts warming up. Before continuing, allow for the warmup process to be finished.

Step 3: Get The Materials Ready
Assemble the supplies whilst the Ninja Foodi begins to warm up. This might entail preparing veggies, marinated cuts of meat, or setting up ingredients in the cooking trays.

Step 4: Fill the Baskets
Based on the preparation mode you selected plus the specifics of the technique, put your items in the cooking baskets or on crisping platters. To guarantee sufficient ventilation for equal drying, do not cram the baskets with too many items.

Step 5: Specify your cooking variables
After all of your ingredients are placed into the Ninja Foodi Dual Air Fryer basket, it is necessary to adjust your cooking preferences. Take the following actions:

1. Choose the proper cooking mode.

Adjust the appropriate temperature for cooking with the control panel for temperature. Utilize the standard range if you feel it is appropriate for the meal or consult the instructions for the suggested temperatures.

2. Adjust your cooking duration with the timer. Once more, consult the recipe or adhere to basic instructions for the particular food you are cooking.

Step 6: Cooking Process

Hit the "Start" icon to initiate the cooking procedure after you have set the cooking settings. The cooking phase will start on the Ninja Foodi Dual Air Fryer, while the electronic display will show the running timing.

Step 7: Observe and Rotate

It is indeed an effective strategy to keep an eye on the food as it cooks, particularly if you are utilizing the air-frying feature. To guarantee uniform browning and crispiness, you may be required to turn or toss the components periodically during the cooking process, according to the instructions provided.

Step 8: Assess for completion

Keeping a watchful eye on the food as the process of cooking draws to a close to avoid overcooking is vital. If you want to be sure your meal is cooked to the right degree of completion, you can use a food thermometer or undertake a visual assessment.

Step 9: Plate, Serve, and Dig In

Taking a pair of oven mitts or tongs, gently take your beautifully prepared meal out of the Ninja Foodi Dual Air Fryer since its baskets and platters can be scalding. You are now free to consume your tasty, golden masterpieces after transferring your meal to a serving tray.

Step 10: Cleaning and Maintenance

Once you have enjoyed your supper, you need to scrub the appliance. Take apart the frying baskets and crisper surfaces after making sure everything has cooled. Cleaning up after using these parts is usually simple because they can go in the dishwasher. You can store the device for later use by giving the inside of the equipment a wipe.

Straight from the Store

Investing in and bringing home your new Ninja Foodi Dual Air Fryer is an exciting experience. Once you get it home from the store, it can be very difficult to wait before you can start testing out its features and cooking tasty dishes. However, when brought straight from the store, you need to first ensure you have set it up correctly and know the various functions thoroughly. The following are crucial steps to ensure a safe and exciting cooking experience:

1. Gently unwrap the packaging for your Ninja Foodie Dual Air Fryer and examine every piece before using it. Verify that each component is intact and ensure there are no indications of wear or omitted pieces. This is done by going through the maker's checklists.
2. Study the handbook carefully and spend some time reviewing the instruction manual. This stage is essential for being acquainted with the attributes, operations, and safety regulations of the device. Using the dual-zone technology along with other parameters correctly will be essential to obtaining maximum use possible from your air fryer.
3. Space and Ventilation: Choose a good spot to put your new equipment in the kitchen. To ensure appropriate circulation throughout functioning, use a surface that is sturdy and level and has plenty of ventilation. To maintain optimum circulation, keep it away from cupboards or walls that are too near.
4. Washing and Preparing: Rinse all the detachable components, including the cooking containers, crisper dishes, and extras, in soapy warm water prior to the initial usage. Carefully wash and air-dry everything. Additionally, you should use a moist cloth to wipe the device's inside to get rid of any production messes.
5. First Testing Cycle: Carry out a first trial run without any food. This makes sure the device is in good working order and helps remove any leftover odors or impurities from the production procedure.
6. Learn about Dual-Zone Technologies: Get to know Dual-Zone Innovation, that allows you to concurrently cook two distinct foods with diverse settings. It allows you to program every zone by utilizing the Smart Set feature. This function distinguishes the Ninja Foodi Dual Air Fryer and may significantly simplify the process of preparing meals. Try it out to learn the way it functions and how it may improve how you cook.
7. Attempt Easy dishes: Start your cooking career with dishes that are simple to follow. To gain a sense of how the gadget prepares meals, begin by roasting or air-frying some simple foods. As you grow more used to its functioning, you may progressively progress to more complicated dishes.
8. Upkeep: Follow the directions provided by the manufacturer for cleaning the detachable components and inside of the device after each usage. A clean Ninja Foodi Dual Air Fryer will ensure optimum performance and durability.
9. Look into Recipe materials: The Ninja Foodi Dual Air Fryer has a tonne of recipe materials at your disposal, like cookbooks, internet forums, and webpages. Browse these sites to find original and mouth-watering dishes you can attempt with the latest gadget.
10. Take part in the cooking adventure: Experience the ease and adaptability of the Ninja Foodie Dual Air Fryer. Test out various approaches to cooking and techniques, and then enjoy the mouthwatering outcomes from your gourmet endeavors.

You will be well-equipped to use the Ninja Foodi Dual Air Fryer for an exquisite experience if you stick to these instructions. You can quickly start preparing a variety of delectable dishes and taking advantage of this cutting-edge kitchen gadget thanks to its dual-zone functionality and flexible cooking features.

Cleaning and Caring for Ninja Foodi Dual Air Fryer

To prolong the life of the Ninja Foodi Dual Air Fryer and retain the standard of your food preparation, it is crucial to regularly clean and care for it. You can relish delectable foods hassle-free with regular upkeep. Below are a few detailed instructions for understanding how to maintain and wipe down the appliance:

Taking Care of the Detachable Parts

The Ninja Foodi Dual Air Fryer needs to be constantly unplugged and given time for cooling down prior to cleaning. This keeps mishaps from happening and keeps you protected.

- **Disconnect All Removable Components:** Disconnect all detachable components, including the crisper surfaces, extras, and frying baskets. For simple cleaning, they are normally dishwasher-appropriate. Use a gentle sponge or towel and soapy water that is warm to clean it by hand if you want.
- **Soaking and Scrubbing:** Should you come across tough food leftovers, give the detachable pieces a quick soak in warm water containing soap to

help remove the particles. After that, scrub delicately with a gentle scrubber or sponges. Don't use anything harsh that might harm the nonstick surfaces.
- **Wash and dry:** To get rid of detergent remains, carefully wash each component in fresh water. Before putting them back together or keeping them, make sure they are totally dry. The nonstick coatings are preserved and moisture-related degradation is avoided by drying.

Internal Maintenance
Allow for inside to Cool Off: Prior to washing the device, make sure the inside has had time to cool off. It is additionally suggested to wait for any meals or oil splashes to harden and settle to allow for easy cleanup.
- The Ninja Foodi Dual Air Fryer's inside should be cleaned with a moist cloth or wipe. You can saturate the fabric with a little soapy water to remove very difficult streaks or remnants. Avoid allowing moisture to enter the electrical parts.
- Thorough Cleansing: At times, you might have to do a more in-depth cleansing. To accomplish this, use an equal quantity of water and white vinegar. Wipe the inside carefully using a wet cloth or towel along with this solvent. Dry completely after rinsing with fresh water.

External Maintenance
Make sure that the gadget is disconnected before washing the outside to avoid electrical shocks.
- **Clean up:** To clean the Ninja Foodi Dual Air Fryer's outside areas, utilize a wet towel. Dry thoroughly to avoid water stains or spots.

Maintaining Attachments
- **Safely Store Attachments:** After washing, place the spare parts in a dry, tidy location. For quick access, it is beneficial to store them next to the machine or adjacent.
- **Periodic Inspection:** Check the parts from time to time for damage or deterioration. To preserve the functioning of the device, it is advised to change the non-stick coverings whenever you detect any problems.

More Information for Upkeep and Care
Avoiding Abrasives: Don't clean the Ninja Foodi Dual Air Fryer with stainless steel wool, harsh scrubbing pads, or other strong chemical-based cleaners. They can harm the device's enamel and non-stick features.
Periodic Repair: To guarantee optimal efficiency, carry out routine maintenance procedures, such as inspecting the device's seals, pivots, and warming components for signs of deterioration. Any problems should be resolved right away to avoid future harm.
Ventilation: Make sure there are no obstacles in airflow intake locations or the passageways. The gadget needs enough airflow to operate properly.
Filtration Upkeep: If your device has an air filter, clean it or substitute it in accordance with the directions from its maker. Airflow is maintained and odors are prevented by clean filters.

Prevent Submerging: Never immerse the Ninja Foodi Dual Air Fryer's core component into water or any other kind of fluid. It has electrical parts that should not be exposed to moisture.

Frequently Asked Questions & Notes

1. How challenging is it to keep the Ninja Foodi Dual Air Fryer?
It isn't too difficult to clean the Ninja Foodi Dual Air Fryer. Cooker baskets and crisper discs are a couple of the detachable components that may go into the dishwashers. There is additionally the choice of manual cleaning in warm, soapy water using a fluffy sponge. Food safety is maintained and durability is ensured by regular washing.

2. Are metal utensils compatible with air-frying baskets?
As metallic objects might harm the non-stick surface, it is best to refrain from using them in the basket. Choose silicone, wooden, or plastic kitchenware alternatively to avoid scratches.

3. Could I use the dual-zone technology for cooking two distinct foods at once?
Absolutely. It is possible to jointly prepare two distinct meals at two distinct temperatures with the help of dual-zone technologies and the smart set panel. Using this tool while multitasking in your kitchen is really useful.

4. How can I keep meals from clinging to the dinnerware or serving baskets?
When putting the food into the pans or onto the platters, be certain to gently oil it or apply spray of cooking oil to avoid stickiness. The nonstick coatings can also be kept functional by washing them right away after usage.

5. Is it okay to dehydrate veggies and fruits with the Ninja Foodi Dual Air Fryer?
Indeed. The Ninja Foodi can effectively dehydrate fruits and veggies. Remain patient, though, since dehydration might take a while. For best results, spread the items evenly over the drying trays.

Additional Notes for Best Results:
Security should always come first. Whenever not in use, disconnect the gadget and abide by the security instructions in the user handbook.
Play with Ingredients: To fully utilize the adaptability of the Ninja Foodi Dual Air Fryer, never be afraid to play around with various dishes and ways to cook.
Periodic Service: To maintain your equipment in peak shape and guarantee that food will turn out correctly, periodic upkeep and cleaning are essential.
Find Ideas for Your Recipes: You can find a tonne of websites, cookbooks, and internet forums devoted to Ninja Foodi ideas. These might offer inspiration and direction for your culinary explorations.
Dual Zone: Push the Start or Pause switch to guarantee that the cooking period is completed in synchrony. For additional instructions, read through the manufacturer's instruction manual carefully.

Fundamentals of Ninja Foodi Dual Air Fryer | 5

4-Week Diet Plan

Week 1

Day 1:
Breakfast: Cinnamon Banana Bread with Walnuts
Lunch: Salty Garlicky Mushrooms
Snack: Crispy Breaded Avocado Fries
Dinner: Garlicky Teriyaki Wild Salmon
Dessert: Best Churros

Day 2:
Breakfast: Vanilla Butter Toast
Lunch: Savoury Fried Rice with Peas & Carrots
Snack: Classic Soft Pretzels
Dinner: Buttery Chicken Breast
Dessert: Vanilla Chocolate Cake

Day 3:
Breakfast: Classic Egg in a Hole
Lunch: Healthy Black Beans & Veggie Burgers
Snack: Crispy Spicy Pumpkin Fries
Dinner: Air Fryer Bacon Wrapped Hot Dogs
Dessert: Raisins & Walnuts Semolina Cake

Day 4:
Breakfast: Quick Hard Boiled Eggs
Lunch: Quick Balsamic Asparagus
Snack: Easy Potato Fries
Dinner: Buttery Fried Salmon Fillets
Dessert: Lemon Cheesecake

Day 5:
Breakfast: Easy Baked Bagels
Lunch: Chili Butternut Squash Cubes
Snack: Crispy Spicy Pumpkin Fries
Dinner: Buttery Bagel Crusted Chicken Strips
Dessert: Chocolate Chip Mug Cakes

Day 6:
Breakfast: Fried Apples with Cinnamon Oats
Lunch: Honey Glazed Carrots with Thyme
Snack: Cheese Jalapeño Poppers with Spring Onion
Dinner: Herbs Baked Pork Chops
Dessert: Vanilla Chocolate Cake

Day 7:
Breakfast: Homemade Sesame Yogurt Bagels
Lunch: Spicy Spiced Butter Courgettes
Snack: Crunchy Onion Rings
Dinner: Homemade Breaded Tilapia Fillets
Dessert: Raisins & Walnuts Semolina Cake

Week 2

Day 1:
Breakfast: Vanilla Butter Toast
Lunch: Parmesan Asparagus
Snack: Crispy Breaded Mozzarella Sticks
Dinner: Crunchy Breaded Chicken Breasts
Dessert: Vanilla Chocolate Cake

Day 2:
Breakfast: Quick Hard Boiled Eggs
Lunch: Spicy Crispy Green Tomatoes
Snack: Crispy Lemony Calamari Rings
Dinner: Lemon-Chili Salmon
Dessert: Cherry Crumble

Day 3:
Breakfast: Classic Egg in a Hole
Lunch: Refreshing Balsamic Brussel Sprouts
Snack: Delicious Cheese Beef Taquitos
Dinner: Herbed Garlic Lamb Chops
Dessert: Butter Oats Cookies

Day 4:
Breakfast: Easy Baked Bagels
Lunch: Cheesy Garlic Broccoli
Snack: Salty Fresh Kale Chips
Dinner: Beer-Marinated Duck Breast
Dessert: Raisins & Walnuts Semolina Cake

Day 5:
Breakfast: Homemade Sesame Yogurt Bagels
Lunch: Sticky Tofu in Ginger Orange Sauce
Snack: Homemade Potato Waffle Fries
Dinner: Lemony Herbed Salmon with Asparagus
Dessert: Chocolate Pistachios Muffins

Day 6:
Breakfast: Fried Apples with Cinnamon Oats
Lunch: Traditional Hasselback Potatoes
Snack: Rosemary Cheese Turkey Croquettes
Dinner: Gingered Chicken Drumsticks
Dessert: Chocolate Chip Mug Cakes

Day 7:
Breakfast: Sweet French Toasts
Lunch: Cheese Prawn Salad with Cherry Tomatoes
Snack: Cumin Cauliflower Poppers
Dinner: Simple Taco Seasoned Lamb Chops
Dessert: Lime Mousse

Week 3

Day 1:
Breakfast: Classic Egg in a Hole
Lunch: Traditional Hasselback Potatoes
Snack: Crispy Spicy Pumpkin Fries
Dinner: Crispy Cheese Chicken Tenderloins
Dessert: Best Churros

Day 2:
Breakfast: Cinnamon Banana Bread with Walnuts
Lunch: Salty Garlicky Mushrooms
Snack: Simple Potato Chips
Dinner: Chili-Garlic Lamb Loin Chops
Dessert: Vanilla Chocolate Cake

Day 3:
Breakfast: Easy Baked Bagels
Lunch: Savoury Fried Rice with Peas & Carrots
Snack: Crispy Breaded Mozzarella Sticks
Dinner: Herbed Spicy Whole Chicken
Dessert: Lemon Cheesecake

Day 4:
Breakfast: Fried Apples with Cinnamon Oats
Lunch: Healthy Black Beans & Veggie Burgers
Snack: Fresh Crispy Fried Okra
Dinner: Herbed Beef Roast with Onion
Dessert: Chocolate Pistachios Muffins

Day 5:
Breakfast: Traditional Avocado Egg Cups
Lunch: Cheesy Garlic Broccoli
Snack: Salty Fresh Kale Chips
Dinner: Healthy Fried Salmon with Asparagus
Dessert: Cherry Crumble

Day 6:
Breakfast: Homemade Sesame Yogurt Bagels
Lunch: Sticky Tofu in Ginger Orange Sauce
Snack: Rosemary Cheese Turkey Croquettes
Dinner: Almond Crusted Chicken
Dessert: Butter Brownies

Day 7:
Breakfast: Sweet French Toasts
Lunch: Spicy Spiced Butter Courgettes
Snack: Homemade Potato Waffle Fries
Dinner: Baked Lamb Steaks
Dessert: Lime Mousse

Week 4

Day 1:
Breakfast: Vanilla Butter Toast
Lunch: Parmesan Asparagus
Snack: Crispy Lemony Calamari Rings
Dinner: Garlicky Cumin Chicken Thighs
Dessert: Butter Oats Cookies

Day 2:
Breakfast: Quick Hard Boiled Eggs
Lunch: Spicy Crispy Green Tomatoes
Snack: Delicious Cheese Beef Taquitos
Dinner: Garlicky Fried Salmon Fillets
Dessert: Lemon Cheesecake

Day 3:
Breakfast: Cinnamon Banana Bread with Walnuts
Lunch: Refreshing Balsamic Brussel Sprouts
Snack: Crispy Breaded Avocado Fries
Dinner: Buttery Chicken Breast
Dessert: Cherry Crumble

Day 4:
Breakfast: Lemony Salmon Quiche
Lunch: Cheese Prawn Salad with Cherry Tomatoes
Snack: Cumin Cauliflower Poppers
Dinner: Herbed Garlic Pork Chops
Dessert: Best Churros

Day 5:
Breakfast: Sweet French Toasts
Lunch: Quick Balsamic Asparagus
Snack: Classic Soft Pretzels
Dinner: Crispy Herbed Chicken
Dessert: Butter Brownies

Day 6:
Breakfast: Traditional Avocado Egg Cups
Lunch: Chili Butternut Squash Cubes
Snack: Fresh Crispy Fried Okra
Dinner: Cajun Flank Steak
Dessert: Chocolate Pistachios Muffins

Day 7:
Breakfast: Sweet French Toasts
Lunch: Honey Glazed Carrots with Thyme
Snack: Homemade Potato Waffle Fries
Dinner: Crispy Cajun Cod Fillets
Dessert: Butter Oats Cookies

Chapter 1 Breakfast Recipes

Quick Hard Boiled Eggs

⏰ **Prep:** 5 minutes 🍲 **Cook:** 18 minutes 📚 **Serves:** 6

Preparation:

1. Press your chosen zone - "Zone 1" or "Zone 2" and then rotate the knob to select "Air Fryer".
2. Set the temperature to 120 degrees C, and then set the time for 5 minutes to preheat.
3. After preheating, arrange eggs into the basket of each zone.
4. Slide the baskets into Air Fryer and set the time for 18 minutes.
5. After cooking time is completed, transfer the eggs into cold water and serve.

Serving Suggestions: Top with salt and pepper.
Variation Tip: You can serve with avocado.

Ingredients:
6 eggs
Cold water

Nutritional Information per Serving: Calories: 78 | Fat: 5g | Sat Fat: 1g | Carbohydrates: 1g | Fibre: 0g | Sugar: 1g | Protein: 6g

Classic Egg in a Hole

⏰ **Prep:** 5 minutes 🍲 **Cook:** 8 minutes 📚 **Serves:** 1

Preparation:

1. Line either basket of "Zone 1" and "Zone 2" with a greased piece of foil.
2. Press your chosen zone - "Zone 1" or "Zone 2" and then rotate the knob to select "Air Fryer".
3. Set the temperature to 160 degrees C, and then set the time for 3 minutes to preheat.
4. After preheating, place the butter on both sides of the bread. Cut a hole in the centre of the bread and crack the egg.
5. Slide the basket into the Air Fryer and set the time for 6 minutes.
6. After cooking time is completed, transfer the bread to a serving plate and serve.

Serving Suggestions: Top with salt and pepper.
Variation Tip: You can serve with veggies.

Ingredients:
1 tablespoon butter, softened
2 eggs
2 slices of bread
Salt and black pepper, to taste

Nutritional Information per Serving: Calories: 377 | Fat: 22g | Sat Fat: 10g | Carbohydrates: 28g | Fibre: 2g | Sugar: 4g | Protein: 17g

Cinnamon Banana Bread with Walnuts

⏰ **Prep: 10 minutes** 🍲 **Cook: 35 minutes** 📚 **Serves: 8**

Preparation:

1. Combine flour, cinnamon, nutmeg, baking soda, and salt in a large mixing basin.
2. Mash the banana in a separate dish before adding the eggs, sugar, milk, yoghurt, oil, and vanilla extract.
3. Mix the wet and dry ingredients in a mixing bowl and stir until just combined.
4. Arrange the batter on the loaf pan, top with chopped walnuts.
5. Press either "Zone 1" and "Zone 2" and then rotate the knob select "Air Fryer".
6. Set the temperature to 155 degrees C, and then set the time for 3 minutes to preheat.
7. After preheating, arrange 1 loaf pan into the basket.
8. Slide basket into Air Fryer and set the time for 35 minutes.
9. After cooking time is completed, remove pan from Air Fryer.
10. Place the loaf pan onto a wire rack, cool for about 10 minutes.
11. Carefully invert the bread onto a wire rack to cool completely before slicing
12. Cut the bread into desired-sized slices and serve.

Serving Suggestions: Top with maple syrup.
Variation Tip: You can serve with fruits.

Ingredients:

95g flour
1 teaspoon ground cinnamon
¼ teaspoon ground nutmeg
½ teaspoon salt
¼ teaspoon baking soda
2 medium-sized ripe bananas mashed
2 large eggs lightly beaten
100g granulated sugar
2 tablespoons whole milk
1 tablespoon plain nonfat yoghurt
2 tablespoons vegetable oil
1 teaspoon vanilla
2 tablespoons walnuts roughly chopped

Nutritional Information per Serving: Calories: 186 | Fat: 7g | Sat Fat: 3g | Carbohydrates: 29g | Fibre: 1g | Sugar: 17g | Protein: 4g

Easy Baked Bagels

⏰ **Prep: 10 minutes** 🍲 **Cook: 15 minutes** 📚 **Serves: 4**

Preparation:

1. Combine the self-rising flour and Greek yoghurt in a medium mixing bowl with a wooden spoon.
2. Knead the dough on a lightly floured board, about 5 minutes.
3. Divide the dough into four equal pieces. Roll each piece into a thin rope, securing the ends to form a bagel shape. Sprinkle the sesame seeds on it.
4. Press either "Zone 1" or "Zone 2" and then rotate the knob to select "Air Fryer".
5. Set the temperature to 140 degrees C, and then set the time for 3 minutes to preheat.
6. After preheating, arrange bagels into the basket.
7. Slide basket into Air Fryer and set the time for 15 minutes.
8. After cooking time is completed, remove both pans from Air Fryer.
9. Place the bagels onto a wire rack to cool for about 10 minutes and serve.

Serving Suggestions: Serve with avocado.
Variation Tip: You can skip egg wash.

Ingredients:

125g self-rising flour
240g non-fat plain Greek yoghurt
1 beaten egg
30g sesame seeds

Nutritional Information per Serving: Calories: 148 | Fat: 1g | Sat Fat: 1g | Carbohydrates: 25g | Fibre: 1g | Sugar: 2g | Protein: 10g

Vanilla Butter Toast

🕐 **Prep:** 10 minutes   🍲 **Cook:** 5 minutes   📚 **Serves:** 6

Preparation:

1. Softened butter is mashed with a fork or the back of a spoon, and then sugar, cinnamon, vanilla, and salt are added.
2. Stir everything together thoroughly.
3. Spread one-sixth of the mixture onto each slice of bread, covering the entire surface.
4. Press your chosen zone - "Zone 1" or "Zone 2" and then rotate the knob to select "Air Fryer".
5. Set the temperature to 200 degrees C, and then set the time for 3 minutes to preheat.
6. After preheating, arrange bread into the basket of each zone.
7. Slide the basket into the Air Fryer and set the time for 5 minutes.
8. After cooking time is completed, remove both baskets from Air Fryer.
9. Cut bread slices diagonally and serve.

Serving Suggestions: Serve with maple syrup.
Variation Tip: You can add 2 pinches of black pepper.

Ingredients:

12 slices bread
115g butter, at room temperature
100g white sugar
1½ teaspoons ground cinnamon
1½ teaspoons pure vanilla extract
1 pinch of salt

Nutritional Information per Serving: Calories: 355 | Fat: 17g | Sat Fat: 10g | Carbohydrates: 45g | Fibre: 3g | Sugar: 20g | Protein: 6g

Fried Apples with Cinnamon Oats

🕐 **Prep:** 10 minutes   🍲 **Cook:** 15 minutes   📚 **Serves:** 4

Preparation:

1. Apply the butter to the apple halves' tops.
2. Combine the remaining butter, oats, honey, and cinnamon in a mixing bowl.
3. Distribute the mixture evenly over the apples' tops.
4. Press either "Zone 1" or "Zone 2" and then rotate the knob to select "Air Fryer".
5. Set the temperature to 190 degrees C, and then set the time for 3 minutes to preheat.
6. After preheating, Arrange the apples in the basket.
7. Slide basket into Air Fryer and set the time for 15 minutes.
8. After cooking time is completed, remove basket from Air Fryer.
9. Place them on serving plates and serve.

Serving Suggestions: Top with extra cinnamon sugar.
Variation Tip: You can also top with whipped cream.

Ingredients:

2 apples, cut in half and cored
2 tablespoons butter, melted
40g oats
3 teaspoons honey
½ teaspoon ground cinnamon

Nutritional Information per Serving: Calories: 153 | Fat: 6g | Sat Fat: 1g | Carbohydrates: 24g | Fibre: 3g | Sugar: 14g | Protein: 2g

Traditional Avocado Egg Cups

⏰ Prep: 15 minutes   🍲 Cook: 12 minutes   🍽 Serves: 4

Preparation:

1. Line either basket of "Zone 1" and "Zone 2" of Ninja Foodi 2-Basket Air Fryer with a greased square piece of foil.
2. Press your chosen zone - "Zone 1" and "Zone 2" and then rotate the knob to select "Bake".
3. Set the temperature to 200 degrees C and then set the time for 5 minutes to preheat.
4. Meanwhile, carefully scoop out about 2 teaspoons of flesh from each avocado half.
5. Crack 1 egg in each avocado half and sprinkle with salt and black pepper.
6. After preheating, arrange 2 avocado halves into the basket.
7. Slide the basket into the Air Fryer and set the time for 12 minutes.
8. After cooking time is completed, transfer the avocado halves and onto serving plates and serve hot.

Serving Suggestions: Serve with buttered toasts.
Variation Tip: Don't use over-ripe avocados.

Ingredients:

2 avocados, halved and pitted
4 eggs
Salt and ground black pepper, as required

Nutritional Information per Serving: Calories: 268 | Fat: 24g | Sat Fat: 5.5g | Carbohydrates: 9g | Fibre: 6.7g | Sugar: 0.8g | Protein: 7.5g

Lemony Salmon Quiche

⏰ Prep: 15 minutes   🍲 Cook: 20 minutes   🍽 Serves: 4

Preparation:

1. In a bowl, mix together the salt, black pepper, salmon, and lemon juice. Set aside.
2. In another bowl, add egg yolk, flour, butter, and water and mix until a dough forms.
3. Divide the dough into 2 portions.
4. Place each dough onto a floured smooth surface and roll into about 17.5cm round.
5. Place each rolled dough into a quiche pan and press firmly in the bottom and along the edges.
6. Then trim the excess edges.
7. In a small bowl, add the eggs, salt, cream, and black pepper and beat until well combined.
8. Place the cream mixture over each crust evenly and top with the salmon, followed by the spring onion.
9. Press either "Zone 1" or "Zone 2" of Ninja Foodi 2-Basket Air Fryer and then rotate the knob for each zone to select "Air Fry".
10. Set the temperature to 180 degrees C and then set the time for 5 minutes to preheat.
11. After preheating, arrange 1 quiche pan into the basket of each zone.
12. Slide the basket into the Air Fryer and set the time for 20 minutes.
13. After cooking time is completed, remove the quiche pans from Air Fryer.
14. Cut each quiche in 2 portions and serve hot.

Serving Suggestions: Serve with fresh greens.
Variation Tip: Use skinless salmon fillets.

Ingredients:

275g salmon fillets, chopped
Salt and ground black pepper, as required
1 tablespoon fresh lemon juice
2 egg yolks
7 tablespoons chilled butter
165g flour
2 tablespoons cold water
4 eggs
6 tablespoons whipping cream
2 spring onions, chopped

Nutritional Information per Serving: Calories: 592 | Fat: 39g | Sat Fat: 20.1g | Carbohydrates: 33.8g | Fibre: 1.4g | Sugar: 0.8g | Protein: 27.2

Chapter 1 Breakfast Recipes

Homemade Sesame Yogurt Bagels

⏰ **Prep: 15 minutes** 🍲 **Cook: 12 minutes** 📚 **Serves: 4**

Preparation:

1. In a large bowl, mix together the flour, salt and baking powder.
2. Add the yogurt and mix until a dough ball forms.
3. Arrange the dough onto a lightly floured surface and then cut into 4 equal-sized balls.
4. Roll each ball into a 17 – 19 cm rope and then join ends to shape a bagel.
5. Grease basket of Ninja Foodi 2-Basket Air Fryer.
6. Press your chosen zone - "Zone 1" or "Zone 2" and then rotate the knob to select "Air Fry".
7. Set the temperature to 165 degrees C and then set the time for 5 minutes to preheat.
8. Meanwhile, add egg and water in a small bowl and mix well.
9. Brush the bagels with egg mixture evenly.
10. Sprinkle the top of each bagel with sesame seeds and salt, pressing lightly.
11. After preheating, arrange 2 bagels into the basket of each zone.
12. Slide the basket into the Air Fryer and set the time for 12 minutes.
13. After cooking time is completed, remove the bagels from Air Fryer and serve warm.

Serving Suggestions: Serve with cream cheese.
Variation Tip: Use room temperature eggs.

Ingredients:

125g plain flour
2 teaspoons baking powder
Salt, as required
240g plain Greek yogurt
1 egg, beaten
1 tablespoon water
1 tablespoon sesame seeds
1 teaspoon coarse salt

Nutritional Information per Serving: Calories: 188 | Fat: 3.3g | Sat Fat: 1.2g | Carbohydrates: 29.9g | Fibre: 1.2g | Sugar: 4.5g | Protein: 8.5g

Sweet French Toasts

⏰ **Prep: 15-minutes** 🍲 **Cook: 6minutes** 📚 **Serves: 4e**

Preparation:

1. Line each basket of "Zone 1" and "Zone 2" with a greased piece of foil.
2. Then Press your chosen zone - "Zone 1" or "Zone 2" and then rotate the knob to select "Air Fry".
3. Set the temperature to 200 degrees C and then set the time for 5 minutes to preheat.
4. In a large bowl, pour all ingredients except for bread slices and beat until well combined.
5. Coat the bread slices with egg mixture evenly.
6. After preheating, arrange 4 bread slices into the basket of each zone.
7. Slide the basket into the Air Fryer and set the time for 6 minutes.
8. While cooking, flip the slices once halfway through.
9. After cooking time is completed, remove the French toasts from Air Fryer and serve warm.

Serving Suggestions: Serve with the topping of butter and maple syrup.
Variation Tip: Use thick bread slices.

Ingredients:

4 eggs
120g evaporated milk
6 tables poons sugar
4 teaspoons olive oil
¼ teaspoon ground cinnamon+
¼ teaspoon vanilla extract
8 bread slicest

Nutritional Information per Serving: Calories: 262 | Fat: 12g | Sat Fat: 3.6g | Carbohydrates: 30.8g | Fibre: 0.5g | Sugar: 22.3g | Protein: 9.1g

Chapter 2 Snacks and Starter Recipes

Crispy Spicy Pumpkin Fries

⏰ **Prep: 25 minutes**   🍲 **Cook: 15 minutes**   📚 **Serves: 4**

Preparation:

1. Combine yoghurt, chipotle peppers, and ⅛ teaspoon salt in a small bowl. Refrigerate until ready to serve, covered.
2. Peeled the pumpkin and split it in half lengthwise. Discard the seeds. Cut pumpkin into 1 cm strips.
3. Place in a large mixing bowl. Toss with ½ teaspoon salt, garlic powder, cumin, chili powder, and pepper.
4. Press either "Zone 1" or "Zone 2" and then rotate the knob to select "Air Fry".
5. Set the temperature to 200 degrees C, and then set the time for 5 minutes to preheat.
6. After preheating, spray the Air-Fryer basket with cooking spray and line with parchment paper. Arrange pumpkin fries and spritz cooking spray on them.
7. Slide the basket into the Air Fryer and set the time for 8 minutes.
8. After that, toss them and again cook for 3 minutes longer.
9. After cooking time is completed, transfer them onto serving plates and serve.

Serving Suggestions: Serve with chili sauce.
Variation Tip: You can also add 2 tbsp. maple syrup.

Ingredients:

120g plain Greek yoghurt
2 to 3 teaspoons minced chipotle peppers
⅛ teaspoon plus ½ teaspoon salt, divided
1 medium pie pumpkin
¼ teaspoon garlic powder
¼ teaspoon ground cumin
¼ teaspoon chili powder
¼ teaspoon pepper

Nutritional Information per Serving: Calories: 151 | Fat: 3g | Sat Fat: 2g | Carbohydrates: 31g | Fibre: 2g | Sugar: 12g | Protein: 5g

---

Simple Potato Chips

⏰ **Prep: 5 minutes**   🍲 **Cook: 12 minutes**   📚 **Serves: 2**

Preparation:

1. Potatoes should be washed and dried. Cut them into ½ cm slices.
2. Soak the slices in cold water for 3 minutes to remove the starch.
3. Take the potatoes out of the water and pat them dry. Toss them in a bowl with the olive oil, pepper and a pinch of salt.
4. Press either "Zone 1" or "Zone 2" and then rotate the knob to select "Air Fryer".
5. Set the temperature to 200 degrees C, and then set the time for 5 minutes to preheat.
6. After preheating, arrange potatoes into the basket.
7. Slide the basket into the Air Fryer and set the time for 12 minutes.
8. While cooking, toss the potato pieces once halfway through.
9. After cooking time is completed, transfer the fries onto serving plates and serve.

Serving Suggestions: Serve with any sauce.
Variation Tip: You can sprinkle parsley on top.

Ingredients:

3 medium russet potatoes, sliced
1 teaspoon olive oil
Salt and pepper, to taste

Nutritional Information per Serving: Calories: 272 | Fat: 3g | Sat Fat: 1g | Carbohydrates: 12g | Fibre: 4g | Sugar: 2g | Protein: 7g

Crispy Lemony Calamari Rings

⏰ **Prep:** 5 minutes 🍳 **Cook:** 10 minutes 📚 **Serves:** 4

Preparation:

1. Allow the squid rings to marinade for at least 30 minutes in a bowl with lemon juice. Drain the water in a colander.
2. In a shallow bowl, mix the flour with garlic powder.
3. In a separate bowl, whisk together the egg whites and milk.
4. In a third bowl, combine the salt, panko breadcrumbs, and pepper.
5. Floured first the calamari rings, then dip in the egg mixture, and finally in the panko breadcrumb mixture.
6. Press either "Zone 1" or "Zone 2" and then rotate the knob to select "Air Fry".
7. Set the temperature to 200 degrees C, and then set the time for 5 minutes to preheat.
8. After preheating, spray the Air-Fryer basket with cooking spray and line with parchment paper. Arrange in a single layer and spritz them with cooking spray.
9. Slide the basket into the Air Fryer and set the time for 10 minutes.
10. After cooking time is completed, transfer them onto serving plates and serve.

Serving Suggestions: Serve with chili sauce.
Variation Tip: You can also serve lemon wedges with them.

Ingredients:

455g calamari rings, patted dry
3 tablespoons lemon juice
60g plain flour
1 teaspoon garlic powder
2 egg whites
60ml milk
220g panko breadcrumbs
1½ teaspoon salt
1½ teaspoon ground black pepper

Nutritional Information per Serving: Calories: 591 | Fat: 15g | Sat Fat: 2g | Carbohydrates: 87g | Fibre: 5g | Sugar: 7g | Protein: 26g

Rosemary Cheese Turkey Croquettes

⏰ **Prep:** 20 minutes 🍳 **Cook:** 10 minutes 📚 **Serves:** 6

Preparation:

1. Combine mashed potatoes, rosemary, salt, cheeses, shallot, and pepper in a large mixing bowl; stir in turkey.
2. Lightly but completely combine the ingredients. Form into twelve 2.5cm thick patties.
3. Whisk the egg and water together in a small basin. In a shallow bowl, add the bread crumbs.
4. Dip the croquettes in the egg mixture, then in the bread crumbs, patting them down.
5. Press either "Zone 1" or "Zone 2" and then rotate the knob to select "Air Fry".
6. Set the temperature to 190 degrees C, and then set the time for 5 minutes to preheat.
7. After preheating, spray the Air-Fryer basket with cooking spray and line with parchment paper. Arrange in a single layer and spritz them with cooking spray.
8. Slide the basket into the Air Fryer and set the time for 5 minutes.
9. After that, turn them and again cook for 5 minutes longer.
10. After cooking time is completed, transfer them onto serving plates and serve.

Serving Suggestions: Serve with your favourite sauce.
Variation Tip: You can use any cheese.

Ingredients:

460g mashed potatoes
50g grated Parmesan cheese
50g shredded Swiss cheese
1 shallot, finely chopped
2 teaspoons minced fresh rosemary
½ teaspoon salt
¼ teaspoon pepper
420g finely chopped cooked turkey
1 large egg
2 tablespoons water
110g panko bread crumbs
Cooking spray

Nutritional Information per Serving: Calories: 322 | Fat: 12g | Sat Fat: 6g | Carbohydrates: 22g | Fibre: 2g | Sugar: 2g | Protein: 29g

Chapter 2 Snacks and Starter Recipes

Crispy Breaded Mozzarella Sticks

⏰ **Prep: 10 minutes** 🍲 **Cook: 6 minutes** ≋ **Serves: 6**

Preparation:

1. Remove the crust from the bread. Discard or save for breadcrumbs.
2. Roll the bread into thin slices with a rolling pin.
3. Slice mozzarella into 30 cm x 10 cm -long sticks, nearly the same size as your bread slices.
4. In a small bowl, whisk together the egg and the water.
5. Fill a shallow pie plate halfway with panko.
6. Wrap a bread slice around each mozzarella stick.
7. Brush the egg wash around the edge of the bread and push to seal it. Brush all over the bread outside.
8. Dredge in Panko and push to coat on all sides.
9. Line basket with parchment paper.
10. Press either "Zone 1" or "Zone 2" and then rotate the knob to select "Air Fryer".
11. Set the temperature to 200 degrees C, and then set the time for 5 minutes to preheat.
12. After preheating, arrange sticks into the basket.
13. Slide the basket into the Air Fryer and set the time for 6 minutes.
14. After cooking time is completed, place on a wire rack for a few minutes, then transfer onto serving plates and serve.

Serving Suggestions: Serve with marinara sauce.
Variation Tip: You can use any cheese.

Ingredients:

150g block Mozzarella cheese or string cheese
6 slices of white bread
1 large egg
1 tablespoon water
55g panko breadcrumbs
1 tablespoon olive oil

Nutritional Information per Serving: Calories: 282 | Fat: 6g | Sat Fat: 8g | Carbohydrates: 25g | Fibre: 2g | Sugar: 4g | Protein: 13g

Classic Soft Pretzels

⏰ **Prep: 15 minutes** 🍲 **Cook: 6 minutes** ≋ **Serves: 8**

Preparation:

1. Combine warm water, yeast, sugar, and olive oil in a large mixing bowl. Stir everything together and leave aside for about 5 minutes.
2. Add 375g flour and a teaspoon of salt to the mixture. Stir well.
3. Roll out the dough on a floured surface. Knead for 3 to 5 minutes, or until the dough is no longer sticky, adding 1 tablespoon of flour at a time if necessary.
4. The dough should be divided in half. At a time, work with half of the dough.
5. Each dough half should be divided into eight pieces.
6. Make a 45cm rope out of the dough. Make a U shape out of the dough. Twist the ends two more times.
7. Fold the ends of the dough over the spherical portion.
8. In a small mixing dish, whisk the egg and a tablespoon of water.
9. Brush the egg wash on both sides of the pretzel dough.
10. Press your chosen zone - "Zone 1" or "Zone 2" and then rotate the knob to select "Air Fryer".
11. Set the temperature to 185 degrees C, and then set the time for 5 minutes to preheat.
12. After preheating, arrange pretzels into the basket of each zone.
13. Slide the baskets into Air Fryer and set the time for 6 minutes.
14. After cooking time is completed, place on a wire rack for a few minutes, then transfer onto serving plates and serve.

Serving Suggestions: Serve with any sauce.
Variation Tip: Before air frying, you can sprinkle flake salt over the pretzels.

Ingredients:

360ml warm water
1 tablespoon dry active yeast
1 tablespoon sugar
1 tablespoon olive oil
500g plain flour
1 teaspoon salt
1 large egg
1 tablespoon water

Nutritional Information per Serving: Calories: 450 | Fat: 3g | Sat Fat: 1g | Carbohydrates: 88g | Fibre: 3g | Sugar: 1g | Protein: 15g

Delicious Cheese Beef Taquitos

⏰ **Prep:** 10 minutes 🍲 **Cook:** 6 minutes 📚 **Serves:** 8

Preparation:

1. Season beef mince with salt in a frying pan and cook over medium-high heat.
2. Cook until the meat is nicely browned, stirring frequently and breaking it into fine crumbles. Remove from the heat and drain any remaining grease.
3. Stir in the salsa, garlic, chili powder, cumin, and cheese until all ingredients are completely incorporated, and the cheese has melted.
4. Warm tortillas on a grill or iron frying pan to make them flexible. Allow them to warm rather than crisp and brown.
5. Fill each tortilla with about 1 to 2 tablespoons of the meat mixture and roll it up.
6. Press either "Zone 1" or "Zone 2" and then rotate the knob to select "Air Fryer".
7. Set the temperature to 175 degrees C, and then set the time for 5 minutes to preheat.
8. After preheating, arrange them into the basket.
9. Slide the basket into the Air Fryer and set the time for 6 minutes.
10. After cooking time is completed, place on a wire rack for a few minutes, then transfer onto serving plates and serve.

Serving Suggestions: Serve with ketchup.
Variation Tip: You can use any cheese.

Ingredients:

455g lean beef mince
1 teaspoon salt
70g salsa
½ teaspoon granulated garlic
½ teaspoon chili powder
½ teaspoon cumin
100g shredded cheese
12 mini corn tortillas

Nutritional Information per Serving: Calories: 427 | Fat: 15g | Sat Fat: 6g | Carbohydrates: 49g | Fibre: 7g | Sugar: 1g | Protein: 26g

Fresh Crispy Fried Okra

⏰ **Prep:** 5 minutes 🍲 **Cook:** 10 minutes 📚 **Serves:** 4

Preparation:

1. Wash and trim the ends of the okra before slicing it into 30cm chunks.
2. In a small dish, pour the buttermilk.
3. Combine flour, polenta, salt, and pepper in a separate dish.
4. Coat all sides of okra slices in buttermilk and then in flour mixture.
5. Place a baking sheet on the baskets.
6. Press either "Zone 1" or "Zone 2" and then rotate the knob to select "Air Fryer".
7. Set the temperature to 175 degrees C, and then set the time for 5 minutes to preheat.
8. After preheating, arrange them into the basket.
9. Slide the basket into the Air Fryer and set the time for 8 minutes.
10. After cooking time is completed, place on a wire rack for a few minutes, then transfer onto serving plates and serve.

Serving Suggestions: Season with salt.
Variation Tip: You can also use chili flakes.

Ingredients:

455g fresh okra
240ml buttermilk
125g plain flour
160g polenta
1 teaspoon salt
1 teaspoon fresh ground pepper

Nutritional Information per Serving: Calories: 275 | Fat: 2g | Sat Fat: 1g | Carbohydrates: 56g | Fibre: 6g | Sugar: 6g | Protein: 10g

Homemade Potato Waffle Fries

⏰ **Prep: 10 minutes** 🍲 **Cook: 15 minutes** 📚 **Serves: 2**

Preparation:

1. If desired, peel the potatoes.
2. With Wave-Waffle Cutter, slice potatoes by turning them one-quarter turn after each pass over the blade.
3. In a mixing dish, toss the potato pieces with the seasoning salt. Toss the potatoes in the seasoning to ensure that it is uniformly distributed.
4. Place a baking sheet on the baskets.
5. Press either "Zone 1" or "Zone 2" and then rotate the knob to select "Air Fryer".
6. Set the temperature to 200 degrees C, and then set the time for 5 minutes to preheat.
7. After preheating, arrange them into the basket.
8. Slide the basket into the Air Fryer and set the time for 15 minutes.
9. After cooking time is completed, place on a wire rack for a few minutes, then transfer onto serving plates and serve.

Serving Suggestions: Serve with any sauce.
Variation Tip: You can also sprinkle parsley on top.

Ingredients:

2 russet potatoes
½ teaspoon seasoning salt

Nutritional Information per Serving: Calories: 164 | Fat: 0.2g | Sat Fat: 1g | Carbohydrates: 37g | Fibre: 4g | Sugar: 2g | Protein: 5g

Crunchy Onion Rings

⏰ **Prep: 15 minutes** 🍲 **Cook: 10 minutes** 📚 **Serves: 4**

Preparation:

1. Separate the onion slices into rings.
2. In a shallow dish, mix together the baking powder, flour, and salt.
3. In a second dish, add milk and egg and beat lightly.
4. In a third dish, place the breadcrumbs.
5. Coat each onion ring with flour mixture, then dip into egg mixture, and coat with the breadcrumbs.
6. Lightly Grease basket of Ninja Foodi 2-Basket Air Fryer.
7. Press your chosen zone - "Zone 1" or "Zone 2" and then rotate the knob to select "Air Fry".
8. Set the temperature to 180 degrees C and then set the time for 5 minutes to preheat.
9. After preheating, arrange the onion rings into the basket of each zone.
10. Slide the basket into the Air Fryer and set the time for 10 minutes.
11. After cooking time is completed, remove the onion rings and apples from Air Fryer and serve hot.

Serving Suggestions: Serve with your favourite dipping sauce.
Variation Tip: Cut onion into equal-sized rings.

Ingredients:

1 large onion, cut into ½ cm slices
155g plain flour
1 teaspoon baking powder
Salt, as required
240ml milk
1 egg
75g dry breadcrumbs

Nutritional Information per Serving: Calories: 285 | Fat: 3.8g | Sat Fat: 1.4g | Carbohydrates: 51.6g | Fibre: 2.8g | Sugar: 5.8g | Protein: 2.5g

Salty Fresh Kale Chips

⏱ **Prep: 15 minutes**   🍲 **Cook: 3 minutes**   📚 **Serves: 4**

Preparation:

1. Pour all the ingredients in a large bowl and mix well.
2. Grease basket of Ninja Foodi 2-Basket Air Fryer.
3. Press your chosen zone - "Zone 1" or "Zone 2" and then rotate the knob to select "Air Fry".
4. Set the temperature to 200 degrees C and then set the time for 5 minutes to preheat.
5. After preheating, arrange the kale pieces into the basket of each zone.
6. Slide the basket into the Air Fryer and set the time for 3 minutes.
7. While cooking, toss the kale pieces once halfway through.
8. After cooking time is completed, remove the kale chips and baking pans from Air Fryer.
9. Place the kale chips onto a wire rack to cool for about 10 minutes before serving.

Serving Suggestions: Serve with the sprinkling of coarse salt.
Variation Tip: Pat dry the kale leaves before using.

Ingredients:

1 head fresh kale, stems and ribs removed and cut into 4cm pieces
1 tablespoon olive oil
1 teaspoon soy sauce
⅛ teaspoon cayenne pepper
Pinch of freshly ground black pepper

Nutritional Information per Serving: Calories: 55 | Fat: 3.5g | Sat Fat: 0.5g | Carbohydrates: 5.3g | Fibre: 0.8g | Sugar: 0g | Protein: 1.6g

Cumin Cauliflower Poppers

⏱ **Prep: 15 minutes**   🍲 **Cook: 20 minutes**   📚 **Serves: 6**

Preparation:

1. Press "Zone 1" and "Zone 2" of Ninja Foodi 2-Basket Air Fryer and then rotate the knob for each zone to select "Bake".
2. Set the temperature to 230 degrees C and then set the time for 5 minutes to preheat.
3. In a bowl, place all ingredients and toss to coat well.
4. Divide the cauliflower mixture into 2 greased baking pans.
5. After preheating, arrange 1 baking pan into the basket of each zone.
6. Slide the basket into the Air Fryer and set the time for 20 minutes.
7. While cooking, flip the cauliflower mixture once halfway through.
8. After cooking time is completed, remove the baking pans from Air Fryer and serve the cauliflower poppers warm.

Serving Suggestions: Serve with the garnishing of parsley.
Variation Tip: Cut the cauliflower into uniform-sized florets.

Ingredients:

3 tablespoons olive oil
1 teaspoon paprika
⅛ teaspoon cayenne pepper
½ teaspoon ground cumin
¼ teaspoon ground turmeric
Salt and ground black pepper, as required
1 medium head cauliflower, cut into florets

Nutritional Information per Serving: Calories: 73 | Fat: 7.2g | Sat Fat: 1g | Carbohydrates: 2.7g | Fibre: 1.3g | Sugar: 1.1g | Protein: 1g

Crispy Breaded Avocado Fries

⏰ Prep: 15 minutes 🍲 Cook: 10 minutes 📚 Serves: 8

Preparation:

1. In a shallow bowl, mix together the flour, salt, and black pepper.
2. In a second bowl, place in the egg and water and beat well.
3. In a third bowl, place the breadcrumbs.
4. Coat the avocado slices with flour mixture, then dip into egg mixture and finally, and coat evenly with the breadcrumbs.
5. Now, spray the avocado slices with cooking spray evenly.
6. Grease one basket of Ninja Foodi 2-Basket Air Fryer.
7. Press either "Zone 1" and "Zone 2" and then rotate the knob to select "Air Fry".
8. Set the temperature to 200 degrees C and then set the time for 5 minutes to preheat.
9. After preheating, arrange the avocado slices into the basket.
10. Slide basket into Air Fryer and set the time for 10 minutes.
11. After cooking time is completed, remove the fries from Air Fryer and serve warm.

Serving Suggestions: Serve with yogurt dip.
Variation Tip: Don't use over-ripe avocados.

Ingredients:

60g plain flour
Salt and ground black pepper, as required
2 eggs
1 teaspoon water
100g seasoned breadcrumbs
2 avocados, peeled, pitted and sliced into 8 pieces
Non-stick cooking spray

Nutritional Information per Serving: Calories: 202 | Fat: 12.7g | Sat Fat: 2.4g | Carbohydrates: 18.9g | Fibre: 4.1g | Sugar: 0.4g | Protein: 4.6g

Easy Potato Fries

⏰ Prep: 15 minutes 🍲 Cook: 16 minutes 📚 Serves: 4

Preparation:

1. Lightly Grease basket of Ninja Foodi 2-Basket Air Fryer.
2. Press your chosen zone - "Zone 1" or "Zone 2" and then rotate the knob to select "Air Fry".
3. Set the temperature to 200 degrees C and then set the time for 5 minutes to preheat.
4. In a large bowl, add all the ingredients and toss to coat well.
5. After preheating, arrange the potato sticks into the basket of each zone.
6. Slide the basket into the Air Fryer and set the time for 16 minutes.
7. While cooking, flip the potato sticks once halfway through.
8. After cooking time is completed, remove the potato fries from Air Fryer and serve warm.

Serving Suggestions: Serve with your favourite sauce.
Variation Tip: Soak the potato wedges for about half an hour in cold tap water.

Ingredients:

455g potatoes, peeled and cut into 1cm thick sticks lengthwise
2 tablespoons olive oil
Salt and ground black pepper, as required

Nutritional Information per Serving: Calories: 138 | Fat: 7.1g | Sat Fat: 1g | Carbohydrates: 17.8g | Fibre: 2.7g | Sugar: 1.3g | Protein: 1.9g

Cheese Jalapeño Poppers with Spring Onion

Prep: 15 minutes **Cook: 13 minutes** **Serves: 6**

Preparation:

1. Carefully cut off one-third of each pepper lengthwise and then scoop out the seeds and membranes.
2. In a bowl, mix together the cream cheese, spring onion, coriander, spices and salt.
3. Stuff each pepper with the cream cheese mixture and top with cheese.
4. Grease basket of Ninja Foodi 2-Basket Air Fryer.
5. Press your chosen zone - "Zone 1" or "Zone 2" and then rotate the knob to select "Air Fry".
6. Set the temperature to 200 degrees C and then set the time for 5 minutes to preheat.
7. After preheating, arrange the jalapeño peppers into the basket of each zone.
8. Slide the basket into the Air Fryer and set the time for 13 minutes.
9. After cooking time is completed, remove the jalapeño poppers from Air Fryer and serve immediately.

Serving Suggestions: Serve with the dipping sauce of your choice.
Variation Tip: Use room temperature cream cheese.

Ingredients:

12 large jalapeño peppers
200g cream cheese, softened
25g spring onion, chopped
5g fresh coriander, chopped
¼ teaspoon onion powder
¼ teaspoon garlic powder
Salt, as required
35g sharp cheddar cheese, grated

Nutritional Information per Serving: Calories: 171 | Fat: 15.7g | Sat Fat: 9.7g | Carbohydrates: 3.7g | Fibre: 1.3g | Sugar: 1.2g | Protein: 4.9g

Chapter 3 Vegetables and Sides Recipes

Sweet Buttery Squash slices

⏰ **Prep:** 15 minutes 🍲 **Cook:** 15 minutes 📚 **Serves:** 6

Preparation:

1. Cut the squash in half lengthwise and remove the seeds. Cut each half into 1cm slices.
2. Press your chosen zone - "Zone 1" or "Zone 2" and then rotate the knob to select "Air Fry".
3. Set the temperature to 200 degrees C, and then set the time for 5 minutes to preheat.
4. After preheating, spray the Air-Fryer basket of each zone with cooking spray and place slices in a single layer.
5. Slide the basket into the Air Fryer and set the time for 5 minutes.
6. Carefully turn them and cook for 5 more minutes.
7. Combine sugar and butter; spread over squash and cook 3 minutes longer.
8. After cooking time is completed, serve avocado slices in tortillas with kale mix, tomato, and additional minced coriander and place them on a serving plate and serve.

Serving Suggestions: Sprinkle parsley on top.
Variation Tip: You can add more chopped veggies.

Ingredients:

2 medium butternut squash
130g packed brown sugar
115g butter, softened

Nutritional Information per Serving: Calories: 320 | Fat: 16g | Sat Fat: 10g | Carbohydrates: 48g | Fibre: 3g | Sugar: 29g | Protein: 2g

Parmesan Asparagus

⏰ **Prep:** 5 minutes 🍲 **Cook:** 8 minutes 📚 **Serves:** 4

Preparation:

1. Clean the asparagus and dry it. To remove the woody stalks, cut 2.5cm off the bottom.
2. Place asparagus in a single layer in the air fryer and spray with oil.
3. On top of the asparagus, evenly sprinkle garlic salt. Season with the pepper and salt, then sprinkle with the Parmesan cheese.
4. Press either "Zone 1" or "Zone 2" and then rotate the knob to select "Air Fryer".
5. Set the temperature to 200 degrees C, and then set the time for 5 minutes to preheat.
6. After preheating, arrange them into the basket.
7. Slide the basket into the Air Fryer and set the time for 8 minutes.
8. After cooking time is completed, transfer onto serving plates and serve.

Serving Suggestions: Sprinkle parsley on top.
Variation Tip: You can use powdered or grated cheese.

Ingredients:

1 bundle asparagus
1 teaspoon olive oil
⅛ teaspoon garlic salt
1 tablespoon Parmesan cheese
Pepper, to taste

Nutritional Information per Serving: Calories: 18 | Fat: 2g | Sat Fat: 9g | Carbohydrates: 1g | Fibre: 0g | Sugar: 0g | Protein: 1g

Quick Balsamic Asparagus

⏰ **Prep:** 10 minutes　🍲 **Cook:** 6 minutes　📚 **Serves:** 6

Preparation:

1. Grease basket of Ninja Foodi 2-Basket Air Fryer.
2. Press your chosen zone - "Zone 1" or "Zone 2" and then rotate the knob to select "Air Fry".
3. Set the temperature to 200 degrees C and then set the time for 5 minutes to preheat.
4. In a bowl, mix together the asparagus, oil, vinegar, salt, and black pepper.
5. After preheating, arrange the asparagus into the basket of each zone.
6. Slide the basket into the Air Fryer and set the time for 6 minutes.
7. After cooking time is completed, remove the asparagus from Air Fryer and serve hot.

Serving Suggestions: Serve with the topping of Parmesan cheese.
Variation Tip: You can use butter instead of oil.

Ingredients:

675g asparagus
4 tablespoons olive oil
3 tablespoon balsamic vinegar
Salt and ground black pepper, as required

Nutritional Information per Serving: Calories: 104 | **Fat:** 9.5g | **Sat Fat:** 1.4g | **Carbohydrates:** 4.5g | **Fibre:** 2.4g | **Sugar:** 2.2g | **Protein:** 2.5g

Spicy Crispy Green Tomatoes

⏰ **Prep:** 15 minutes　🍲 **Cook:** 7 minutes　📚 **Serves:** 4

Preparation:

1. Slice the green tomatoes into ½ cm slices and generously coat with salt. Allow for at least 5 minutes of resting time.
2. Put the flour in one bowl, the egg (whisked) in the second, and the breadcrumbs, polenta, paprika, and cayenne pepper in the third bowl to make a breading station.
3. Using a paper towel, pat green tomato slices dry.
4. Dip each tomato slice into the flour, the egg, and finally the polenta mixture, making sure the tomato slices are completely covered.
5. Press either "Zone 1" or "Zone 2" and then rotate the knob to select "Air Fryer".
6. Set the temperature to 195 degrees C, and then set the time for 5 minutes to preheat.
7. After preheating, arrange them into the basket.
8. Slide the basket into the Air Fryer and set the time for 8 minutes.
9. After cooking time is completed, transfer onto serving plates and serve.

Serving Suggestions: Serve with marinara sauce.
Variation Tip: You can also use cayenne pepper.

Ingredients:

3-4 green tomatoes
½ teaspoon salt
65g flour
2 eggs
50g polenta
35g breadcrumbs
⅛ teaspoon paprika
Cayenne pepper

Nutritional Information per Serving: Calories: 186 | **Fat:** 4g | **Sat Fat:** 1g | **Carbohydrates:** 31g | **Fibre:** 4g | **Sugar:** 4g | **Protein:** 8g

Salty Garlicky Mushrooms

⏱ **Prep: 10 minutes**   🍲 **Cook: 10 minutes**   📚 **Serves: 2**

Preparation:

1. To begin, clean the mushrooms. To clean them, use a moist kitchen towel to wipe them down.
2. Avoid getting wet or rushing in the water. Remove the stems from the mushrooms and cut them in half.
3. Season mushrooms with garlic powder, salt, and pepper, and toss with olive oil and soy sauce.
4. Press either "Zone 1" or "Zone 2" and then rotate the knob to select "Bake".
5. Set the temperature to 200 degrees C and then set the time for 5 minutes to preheat.
6. After preheating, arrange them into the basket.
7. Slide the basket into the Air Fryer and set the time for 10 minutes.
8. After cooking time is completed, transfer onto serving plates and serve.

Serving Suggestions: Serve with lemon wedges.
Variation Tip: You can also sprinkle parsley on top.

Ingredients:

200g Bella mushroom cut into half
1 tablespoon olive oil
½ teaspoon garlic powder
1 teaspoon soy sauce
Salt and pepper, to taste

Nutritional Information per Serving: Calories: 92 | Fat: 7g | Sat Fat: 1g | Carbohydrates: 6g | Fibre: 1g | Sugar: 2g | Protein: 3g

Refreshing Balsamic Brussel Sprouts

⏱ **Prep: 10 minutes**   🍲 **Cook: 10 minutes**   📚 **Serves: 2**

Preparation:

1. Brussels sprouts should be rinsed and dried with a kitchen towel.
2. Trim the bottom of each Brussels sprout's hard stem with a sharp knife and cut each Brussels sprout in half lengthwise, from tip to trimmed end.
3. In a medium mixing dish, place the Brussel sprouts. Season with the garlic powder, salt, and pepper. Then drizzle with the olive oil and balsamic vinegar.
4. Toss them in the seasoning until they're evenly covered. It's best to do this using your hands.
5. Press either "Zone 1" or "Zone 2" and then rotate the knob to select "Bake".
6. Set the temperature to 200 degrees C, and then set the time for 5 minutes to preheat.
7. After preheating, arrange them into the basket.
8. Slide the basket into the Air Fryer and set the time for 15 minutes.
9. After cooking time is completed, transfer onto serving plates and serve.

Serving Suggestions: Serve with lemon wedges.
Variation Tip: You can also sprinkle parsley on top.

Ingredients:

455g Brussels sprouts, trimmed and halved
1 tablespoon extra-virgin olive oil
½ teaspoon garlic powder
1 tablespoon balsamic vinegar
¼ teaspoon salt, to taste
⅛ teaspoon black pepper

Nutritional Information per Serving: Calories: 85 | Fat: 4g | Sat Fat: 1g | Carbohydrates: 11g | Fibre: 4g | Sugar: 3g | Protein: 4g

Chili Butternut Squash Cubes

⏰ **Prep: 10 minutes**   🍲 **Cook: 20 minutes**   📚 **Serves: 2**

Preparation:

1. For consistent and speedy cooking, peel and cut the butternut squash into 1.5cm chunks.
2. Place the butternut squash in a mixing dish. Season with garlic powder, salt, chili flakes, and pepper and drizzle with olive oil.
3. Toss them well so that the spice is evenly distributed.
4. Press either "Zone 1" or "Zone 2" and then rotate the knob to select "Bake".
5. Set the temperature to 200 degrees C, and then set the time for 5 minutes to preheat.
6. After preheating, arrange them into the basket,
7. Slide the basket into the Air Fryer and set the time for 25 minutes.
8. After cooking time is completed, transfer onto serving plates and serve.

Serving Suggestions: Serve with lemon wedges.
Variation Tip: You can also sprinkle parsley on top.

Ingredients:

1 small butternut squash, peeled and cut into 1.5cm cubes
1 tablespoon extra-virgin olive oil
½ teaspoon garlic powder
½ teaspoon salt
⅛ teaspoon freshly ground black pepper
1 teaspoon chili flakes

Nutritional Information per Serving: Calories: 148 | Fat: 7g | Sat Fat: 1g | Carbohydrates: 22g | Fibre: 4g | Sugar: 4g | Protein: 2g

Cheesy Garlic Broccoli

⏰ **Prep: 7 minutes**   🍲 **Cook: 5 minutes**   📚 **Serves: 2**

Preparation:

1. Combine the broccoli, olive oil, cheese, and garlic in a container with a cover and shake until equally coated.
2. Any remaining cheese should be pressed into the broccoli florets. To taste, season with salt and pepper.
3. Press either "Zone 1" or "Zone 2" and then rotate the knob to select "Air Fryer".
4. Set the temperature to 200 degrees C, and then set the time for 5 minutes to preheat.
5. After preheating, arrange them into the basket.
6. Slide the basket into the Air Fryer and set the time for 5 minutes.
7. After cooking time is completed, transfer onto serving plates and serve.

Serving Suggestions: Serve with coriander on top.
Variation Tip: You can use any cheese.

Ingredients:

225g broccoli washed, dried, and cut into bite-sized pieces
1 tablespoon olive oil
1 tablespoon parmesan cheese grated
1 clove garlic minced
Salt & pepper, to taste

Nutritional Information per Serving: Calories: 112 | Fat: 8g | Sat Fat: 1g | Carbohydrates: 8g | Fibre: 3g | Sugar: 2g | Protein: 4g

Spicy Spiced Butter Courgettes

⏱ **Prep: 10 minutes**   🍲 **Cook: 15 minutes**   ≋ **Serves: 6**

Preparation:

1. Grease basket of Ninja Foodi 2-Basket Air Fryer.
2. Press your chosen zone - "Zone 1" or "Zone 2" and then rotate the knob to select "Air Fry".
3. Set the temperature to 200 degrees C and then set the time for 5 minutes to preheat.
4. In a large bowl, place in all ingredients and mix well.
5. After preheating, arrange the courgette slices into the basket of each zone.
6. Slide the basket into the Air Fryer and set the time for 15 minutes.
7. After cooking time is completed, remove the squash chunks from Air Fryer.
8. Transfer the courgette slices onto a platter and serve hot.

Serving Suggestions: Serve with the drizzling of lemon juice.
Variation Tip: You can use yellow squash instead of courgette too.

Ingredients:

675g courgettes, sliced
2 tablespoons butter, melted
½ teaspoon dried rosemary, crushed
½ teaspoon ground cumin
½ teaspoon ground coriander
½ teaspoon cayenne pepper
Salt and ground black pepper, as required

Nutritional Information per Serving: Calories: 54 | Fat: 4.1g | Sat Fat: 25g | Carbohydrates: 4g | Fibre: 1.4g | Sugar: 2g | Protein: 1.5g

Savoury Fried Rice with Peas & Carrots

⏱ **Prep: 15 minutes**   🍲 **Cook: 18 minutes**   ≋ **Serves: 8**

Preparation:

1. In a large bowl, add the oil, rice, 1 teaspoon of sesame oil, water, salt, and white pepper and mix well.
2. Divide the rice mixture into 2 lightly greased baking pans.
3. Press "Zone 1" and "Zone 2" of Ninja Foodi 2-Basket Air Fryer and then rotate the knob for each zone to select "Air Fry".
4. Set the temperature to 195 degrees C and then set the time for 5 minutes to preheat.
5. After preheating, arrange 1 baking pan into the basket of each zone.
6. Slide the basket into the Air Fryer and set the time for 18 minutes.
7. While cooking, stir the rice mixture once after 5 minutes.
8. After 12 minutes of cooking, place the beaten egg over rice.
9. After 15 minutes of cooking, stir in the peas and carrots into each pan.
10. Meanwhile, in a bowl, mix together soy sauce, Sriracha sauce, sesame seeds and the remaining sesame oil.
11. After cooking time is completed, remove the baking pans from Air Fryer and transfer the rice mixture into a serving bowl.
12. Drizzle with the sauce and serve.

Serving Suggestions: Serve with the drizzling of lemon juice.
Variation Tip: You can use veggies of your choice.

Ingredients:

500g cooked white rice
1 tablespoon vegetable oil
2 teaspoons sesame oil, toasted and divided
1 tablespoon water
Salt and ground white pepper, as required
1 large egg, lightly beaten
85g frozen peas, thawed
55g frozen carrots, thawed
1 teaspoon Sriracha sauce
1 teaspoon soy sauce
½ teaspoon of toasted sesame seeds

Nutritional Information per Serving: Calories: 438 | Fat: 8.6g | Sat Fat: 1.7g | Carbohydrates: 78g | Fibre: 2.7g | Sugar: 1.9g | Protein: 9.5g

Healthy Black Beans & Veggie Burgers

⏰ **Prep: 15 minutes**   🍲 **Cook: 15 minutes**   📚 **Serves: 8**

Preparation:

1. In a large bowl, add the beans, potatoes, spinach, mushrooms, and seasoning and with your hands, mix until well combined.
2. Make 8 equal-sized patties from the mixture.
3. Spray the patties with cooking spray evenly.
4. Grease basket of Ninja Foodi 2-Basket Air Fryer.
5. Press your chosen zone - "Zone 1" or "Zone 2" and then rotate the knob to select "Air Fry".
6. Set the temperature to 185 degrees C and then set the time for 5 minutes to preheat.
7. After preheating, arrange 4 patties into the basket of each zone.
8. Slide the basket into the Air Fryer and set the time for 12 minutes.
9. After cooking time is completed, remove the patties from Air Fryer.
10. Serve hot.

Serving Suggestions: Serve with fresh greens.
Variation Tip: Feel free to use seasoning of your choice.

Ingredients:

330g cooked black beans
560g boiled potatoes, peeled and mashed
60g fresh spinach, chopped
175g fresh mushrooms, chopped
4 teaspoons Chile lime seasoning
Olive oil cooking spray

Nutritional Information per Serving: Calories: 113 | Fat: 0.4g | Sat Fat: 0g | Carbohydrates: 23.1g | Fibre: 6.2g | Sugar: 1.7g | Protein: 6g

Sticky Tofu in Ginger Orange Sauce

⏰ **Prep: 15 minutes**   🍲 **Cook: 10 minutes**   📚 **Serves: 4**

Preparation:

1. In a bowl, add the tofu, cornflour, and tamari and toss to coat well.
2. Set the tofu aside to marinate for at least 15 minutes.
3. Grease basket of Ninja Foodi 2-Basket Air Fryer.
4. Press either "Zone 1" or "Zone 2" and then rotate the knob to select "Air Fry".
5. Set the temperature to 200 degrees C, and then set the time for 5 minutes to preheat.
6. After preheating, arrange tofu cubes into the basket.
7. Slide basket into Air Fryer and set the time for 10 minutes.
8. Flip the tofu cubes once halfway through.
9. Meanwhile, for the sauce: in a small pan, add all the ingredients over medium-high heat and bring to a boil, stirring continuously.
10. Remove from heat and transfer the sauce into a serving bowl.
11. After cooking time is completed, remove the tofu cubes from Air Fryer.
12. Place the tofu cubes into the bowl with sauce and gently stir to combine.
13. Serve immediately.

Serving Suggestions: Serve with the garnishing of spring onion greens.
Variation Tip: For best result, use freshly squeezed orange juice.

Ingredients:

For Tofu:
455g extra-firm tofu, pressed, drained and cubed
1 tablespoon cornflour
1 tablespoon tamari
For Sauce:
120ml water
80ml fresh orange juice
1 tablespoon maple syrup
1 teaspoon orange zest, grated
1 teaspoon garlic, minced
1 teaspoon fresh ginger, minced
2 teaspoons cornflour
¼ teaspoon red pepper flakes, crushed

Nutritional Information per Serving: Calories: 147 | Fat: 6.7g | Sat Fat: 0.6g | Carbohydrates: 12.7g | Fibre: 0.7g | Sugar: 6.7g | Protein: 12.1g

Honey Glazed Carrots with Thyme

⏱ **Prep: 15 minutes**   🍲 **Cook: 12 minutes**   📚 **Serves: 6**

Preparation:

1. Grease basket of Ninja Foodi 2-Basket Air Fryer.
2. Press your chosen zone - "Zone 1" or "Zone 2" and then rotate the knob to select "Air Fry".
3. Set the temperature to 200 degrees C and then set the time for 5 minutes to preheat.
4. In a bowl, place all ingredients and toss to coat well.
5. After preheating, arrange the carrot chunks into the basket of each zone.
6. Slide the basket into the Air Fryer and set the time for 12 minutes.
7. After cooking time is completed, remove carrot chunks from Air Fryer.
8. Cut each carrot chunks into half and serve hot.

Serving Suggestions: Serve with the topping of fresh herbs.
Variation Tip: Honey can be replaced with maple syrup.

Ingredients:

440g carrots, peeled and cut into large chunks
2 tablespoons olive oil
2 tablespoons honey
1 tablespoon fresh thyme, chopped finely
Salt and ground black pepper, as required

Nutritional Information per Serving: Calories: 93 | Fat: 4.7g | Sat Fat: 0.7g | Carbohydrates: 13.3g | Fibre: 2g | Sugar: 9.4g | Protein: 0.7g

Traditional Hasselback Potatoes

⏱ **Prep: 10 minutes**   🍲 **Cook: 30 minutes**   📚 **Serves: 8**

Preparation:

1. With a sharp knife, cut slits along each potato the short way about ½ cm apart, ensuring slices should stay connected at the bottom.
2. Grease basket of Ninja Foodi 2-Basket Air Fryer.
3. Press your chosen zone - "Zone 1" or "Zone 2" and then rotate the knob to select "Air Fry".
4. Set the temperature to 180 degrees C and then set the time for 5 minutes to preheat.
5. After preheating, arrange 4 potatoes into the basket of each zone.
6. Slide the basket into the Air Fryer and set the time for 30 minutes.
7. After 15 minutes of cooking, coat the potatoes with oil.
8. After cooking time is completed, remove the baking pan of potatoes from Air Fryer and serve immediately.

Serving Suggestions: Serve with the topping of parmesan cheese.
Variation Tip: Use equal-sized potatoes.

Ingredients:

8 potatoes
4 tablespoons olive oil

Nutritional Information per Serving: Calories: 207 | Fat: 7.2g | Sat Fat: 1.1g | Carbohydrates: 33.5g | Fibre: 5.1g | Sugar: 2.5g | Protein: 3.6

Chapter 4 Fish and Seafood Recipes

Cheese Prawn Salad with Cherry Tomatoes

⏰ **Prep:** 15 minutes 🍲 **Cook:** 5 minutes 📚 **Serves:** 4

Preparation:

1. Combine the romaine hearts, tomatoes, and cheese in a large mixing basin; chill until ready to serve.
2. Combine the salt, flour, and pepper in a small bowl. Toss in a few pieces of prawn at a time, tossing to coat; brush off excess.
3. Press your chosen zone - "Zone 1" or "Zone 2" and then rotate the knob to select "Air Fry".
4. Set the temperature to 190 degrees C, and then set the time for 5 minutes to preheat.
5. After preheating, spray the Air-Fryer basket of each zone with the cooking spray, arrange the prawns in a single layer, and spritz them with the cooking spray.
6. Slide the basket into the Air Fryer and set the time for 4 minutes.
7. Carefully turn them and cook 4 minutes longer.
8. After cooking time is completed, toss the romaine mixture with the dressing to coat it, put prawns on top, and place them on a serving plate and serve.

Serving Suggestions: Serve lemon juice on top.
Variation Tip: You can use any salad dressing.

Ingredients:

2 romaine hearts, coarsely chopped
150g cherry tomatoes, halved
25g shredded Parmesan cheese
65g plain flour
¾ teaspoon salt
½ teaspoon pepper
455g uncooked prawns, peeled and deveined
Cooking spray
120g Creamy Caesar Salad Dressing

Nutritional Information per Serving: Calories: 313 | Fat: 21g | Sat Fat: 4g | Carbohydrates: 8g | Fibre: 2g | Sugar: 2g | Protein: 23g

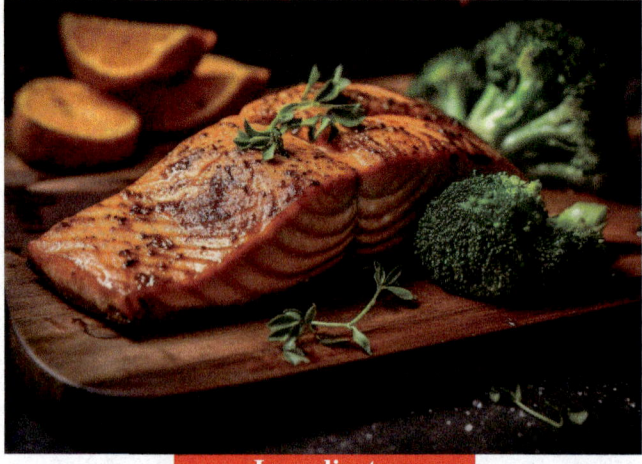

Garlicky Teriyaki Wild Salmon

⏰ **Prep:** 10 minutes 🍲 **Cook:** 5 minutes 📚 **Serves:** 3

Preparation:

1. Whisk everything together to make the marinade.
2. Pour over defrosted fish and marinate for 20 minutes.
3. Press your chosen zone - "Zone 1" or "Zone 2" and then rotate the knob to select "Air Fry".
4. Set the temperature to 175 degrees C, and then set the time for 5 minutes to preheat.
5. After preheating, place a foil sheet on each basket, spray the Air-Fryer basket of each zone with the cooking spray, arrange them in a single layer, and spritz them with the cooking spray.
6. Slide the basket into the Air Fryer and set the time for 12 minutes.
7. Carefully turn them and cook them 6 minutes longer.
8. After cooking time is completed, place them on a serving plate and serve.

Serving Suggestions: Serve with roasted veggies.
Variation Tip: You can also add a teaspoon of red pepper flakes.

Ingredients:

8 tsp Less Sodium Teriyaki
3 tsp honey
2 cubes of frozen garlic
2 tsp extra virgin olive oil
3 pieces of wild salmon

Nutritional Information per Serving: Calories: 198 | Fat: 9g | Sat Fat: 1g | Carbohydrates: 30g | Fibre: 0.1g | Sugar: 27g | Protein: 0.2g

Cheese-Crusted Tuna Patties with Parsley

⏰ **Prep: 10 minutes**   🍳 **Cook: 10 minutes**   📚 **Serves: 3**

Preparation:

1. In a frying pan, heat the oil and butter over medium-high heat.
2. Sauté for 5-7 minutes with the onions, red pepper, and garlic.
3. Drain tuna cans thoroughly. Fill a medium mixing bowl halfway with the mixture. Lime juice should be poured over the tuna.
4. Place sautéed vegetables in a mixing bowl. Combine parsley and cheese in a mixing bowl.
5. Add oregano, salt, and pepper to taste. Add the panko crumbs and mix well.
6. Mix in the eggs until the mixture forms a beautiful Pattie. You can add an extra egg if necessary, although the tuna is usually wet enough that it isn't required.
7. Refrigerate for 30-60 minutes, or even overnight, after forming 6 patties. This will make them more manageable.
8. Remove from the refrigerator and coat in a panko crumb and parmesan cheese mixture.
9. Press your chosen zone - "Zone 1" or "Zone 2" and then rotate the knob to select "Air Fry".
10. Set the temperature to 200 degrees C, and then set the time for 5 minutes to preheat.
11. After preheating, spray the Air-Fryer basket of each zone with the cooking spray, arrange them in a single layer, and spritz them with the cooking spray.
12. Slide the basket into the Air Fryer and set the time for 4 minutes.
13. Carefully turn them and cook 4 minutes longer.
14. After cooking time is completed, place them on a serving plate and serve.

Serving Suggestions: Serve with lemon wedges.
Variation Tip: You can also add a teaspoon of sriracha.

Ingredients:

Tuna Patties
1 tablespoon butter
80g onion chopped
½ red pepper chopped
1 teaspoon minced garlic
2 (175g) cans of tuna fish, drained
1 tablespoon lime juice
15g fresh parsley chopped
3 tablespoons of parmesan cheese grated
½ teaspoon oregano
¼ teaspoon salt
Black pepper to taste
55g panko crumbs
2 eggs whisked
Crumb Coating
55g panko crumbs
25g parmesan cheese
Cooking spray

Nutritional Information per Serving: Calories: 387 | Fat: 17g | Sat Fat: 7g | Carbohydrates: 21g | Fibre: 2g | Sugar: 4g | Protein: 38g

Garlicky Fried Salmon Fillets

⏰ **Prep: 5 minutes**   🍳 **Cook: 0 minutes**   📚 **Serves: 2**

Preparation:

1. Grease basket of Ninja Foodi 2-Basket Air Fryer.
2. Press your chosen zone - "Zone 1" or "Zone 2" and then rotate the knob to select "Air Fry".
3. Set the temperature to 180 degrees C and then set the time for 5 minutes to preheat.
4. Take a bowl, add melted butter, parsley and garlic. Mix together.
5. Season fresh salmon fillets with salt and black pepper.
6. Place the salmon fillets in the butter mixture
7. After preheating, arrange salmon fillets into the basket of each zone.
8. Slide the basket into the Air Fryer and set the time for 10 minutes.
9. After cooking time is completed, remove the salmon fillets from Air Fryer and serve hot.

Serving Suggestions: Serve with the garnishing of spring onion.
Variation Tip: Use skinless salmon fillets.

Ingredients:

2 skin-on salmon fillets
2 garlic cloves, minced
1 teaspoon fresh Italian parsley
2 tablespoons butter, melted
Salt and pepper, to taste

Nutritional Information per Serving: Calories: 107 | Fat: 26.5g | Sat Fat: 10.3g | Carbohydrates: 1g | Fibre: 0.1g | Sugar: 0.1g | Protein: 28.3g

Chapter 4 Fish and Seafood Recipes | 29

Crispy Salmon Cakes with Mayonnaise

⏰ **Prep: 15 minutes**   🍲 **Cook: 0 minutes**   📚 **Serves: 4**

Preparation:

1. In a small mixing dish, combine mayonnaise and Sriracha.
2. To the Sriracha mayo, add the salmon, almond flour, egg, 1½ teaspoons seafood spice, and green onion; pulse quickly for 4 to 5 seconds until ingredients are combined, but small chunks of salmon remain.
3. Spray hands with cooking spray and line a platter with waxed paper. Transfer the salmon mixture to a plate in 8 tiny patties. Refrigerate for about 15 minutes or until cool and stiff.
4. Press your chosen zone - "Zone 1" or "Zone 2" and then rotate the knob to select "Air Fry".
5. Set the temperature to 200 degrees C, and then set the time for 5 minutes to preheat.
6. After preheating, spray the Air-Fryer basket of each zone with the cooking spray, arrange them in a single layer, and spritz them the with cooking spray.
7. Slide the basket into the Air Fryer and set the time for 6 minutes.
8. Carefully turn them and cook them 2 minutes longer.
9. After cooking time is completed, place them on a serving plate and serve.

Serving Suggestions: Garnish with sesame seeds.
Variation Tip: You can also use coconut flour.

Ingredients:

60g mayonnaise
1 tablespoon Sriracha
Salmon Cakes:
455g skinless salmon fillets, cut into 2.5cm pieces
30g almond flour
1 egg, lightly beaten
1 ½ teaspoon seafood seasoning
1 green onion, coarsely chopped
Cooking spray

Nutritional Information per Serving: Calories: 340 | Fat: 24g | Sat Fat: 4g | Carbohydrates: 3g | Fibre: 1g | Sugar: 0.7g | Protein: 25g

Nutritious Honey Glazed Tuna Steaks

⏰ **Prep: 15 minutes**   🍲 **Cook: 6 minutes**   📚 **Serves: 2**

Preparation:

1. Combine the grated ginger, sesame oil, soy sauce, honey, and rice vinegar in a large mixing bowl.
2. Place the tuna steaks in the marinade and leave to marinate in the fridge for 20-30 minutes, covered.
3. Press your chosen zone - "Zone 1" or "Zone 2" and then rotate the knob to select "Air Fry".
4. Set the temperature to 195 degrees C, and then set the time for 5 minutes to preheat.
5. After preheating, spray the Air-Fryer basket of each zone with the cooking spray, arrange the tuna in a single layer, and spritz them with the cooking spray.
6. Slide the basket into the Air Fryer and set the time for 4 minutes.
7. Carefully turn them and cook 2 minutes longer.
8. After cooking time is completed, allow the tuna steaks to rest for a minute or two, then sliced, place them on a serving plate and serve.

Serving Suggestions: Sprinkle green onions on top.
Variation Tip: You can also sprinkle sesame seeds on top.

Ingredients:

2 boneless and skinless yellowfin tuna steaks
60ml soy sauce
2 teaspoons honey
1 teaspoon grated ginger
1 teaspoon sesame oil
½ teaspoon rice vinegar

Nutritional Information per Serving: Calories: 422 | Fat: 23g | Sat Fat: 8g | Carbohydrates: 8g | Fibre: 0g | Sugar: 6g | Protein: 44g

Delicious Cod Cakes with Coriander

⏰ **Prep: 10 minutes**   🍲 **Cook: 0 minutes**   📚 **Serves: 2**

Preparation:

1. Grease basket of Ninja Foodi 2-Basket Air Fryer.
2. Press your chosen zone - "Zone 1" or "Zone 2" and then rotate the knob to select "Air Fry".
3. Set the heat to 200 degrees C and then set the time for 5 minutes to preheat.
4. Take a food processor, add cod fillets and process until crumbly.
5. Take a bowl, add crumbled fish, breadcrumbs, chili sauce, mayo, egg, salt, coriander and pepper. Stir until well combined.
6. Shape the mixture into patties.
7. After preheating, arrange patties into the basket of each zone.
8. Slide the basket into the Air Fryer and set the time for 10 minutes.
9. After cooking time is completed, remove the patties from Air Fryer and serve hot.

Serving Suggestions: Serve with lime wedges.
Variation Tip: Chop the fish finely instead of using a food processor.

Ingredients:

150g cod fillets
55g panko breadcrumbs
1 small egg
1 tablespoon mayonnaise
1 tablespoon sweet chili sauce
1 tablespoon fresh chopped coriander
⅛ teaspoon salt
⅛ teaspoon ground black pepper

Nutritional Information per Serving: Calories: 236 | Fat: 6.9g | Sat Fat: 1.7g | Carbohydrates: 9.1g | Fibre: 0.1g | Sugar: 3.7g | Protein: 18.3g

Buttery Fried Salmon Fillets

⏰ **Prep: 10 minutes**   🍲 **Cook: 0 minutes**   📚 **Serves: 2**

Preparation:

1. Add brown sugar, garlic powder, parsley, salt and pepper in a bowl. Mix well.
2. Place salmon fillets in the mixture and rub generously with it.
3. Meanwhile, Grease basket of Ninja Foodi 2-Basket Air Fryer.
4. Press your chosen zone - "Zone 1" or "Zone 2" and then rotate the knob to select "Air Fry".
5. Set the temperature to 180 degrees C and then set the time for 5 minutes to preheat.
6. After preheating, arrange salmon fillets into the zone 1 and zone 2 of the basket and top them with butter.
7. Slide the basket into the Air Fryer and set the time for 10 minutes.
8. After cooking time is completed, remove the salmon fillets from Air Fryer and serve hot.

Serving Suggestions: Serve with chopped mint leaves on the top.
Variation Tip: Use skinless salmon fillets.

Ingredients:

2 salmon fillets
2 tablespoons butter
1 tablespoon brown sugar
½ teaspoon parsley
½ teaspoon garlic powder
½ teaspoon salt
¼ teaspoon pepper

Nutritional Information per Serving: Calories: 333 | Fat: 17g | Sat Fat: 6.2g | Carbohydrates: 16.7g | Fibre: 0.1g | Sugar: 16.1g | Protein: 29.5g

Tasty Lemony Salmon Fillets

⏰ **Prep:** 10 minutes 🍲 **Cook:** 0 minutes 🗂 **Serves:** 4

Preparation:

1. Grease basket of Ninja Foodi 2-Basket Air Fryer.
2. Press your chosen zone - "Zone 1" or "Zone 2" and then rotate the knob to select "Air Fry".
3. Set the heat to 190 degrees C and then set the time for 5 minutes to preheat.
4. Season the salmon fillets with lemon, salt, garlic powder, black pepper and avocado oil.
5. After preheating, arrange 2 salmon fillets into the basket of each zone.
6. Slide the basket into the Air Fryer and set the time for 10 minutes.
7. After cooking time is completed, remove the salmon fillets from Air Fryer and serve hot.

Serving Suggestions: Serve with chopped parsley on the top.
Variation Tip: Use skin-on salmon fillets.

Ingredients:

2 lemons, zested and sliced
½ teaspoon salt
4 (110g) salmon fillets
1 tablespoon avocado oil
1 teaspoon fresh black pepper
1 teaspoon garlic powder

Nutritional Information per Serving: Calories: 167 | Fat: 7.6g | Sat Fat: 1.1g | Carbohydrates: 3.8g | Fibre: 1.2g | Sugar: 0.9g | Protein: 22.5g

Sweet and Spicy Salmon with Sesame

⏰ **Prep:** 10 minutes 🍲 **Cook:** 2 minutes 🗂 **Serves:** 2

Preparation:

1. In a shallow dish, add soy sauce, salt, pepper and oil. Whisk well.
2. Pour the mixture over salmon-fillets and rub all over the fish.
3. Cover the dish and place the mixture in refrigerator for about 15 minutes.
4. Remove the salmon fillets from refrigerator and shake off the excess marinade.
5. Line each basket of "Zone 1" and "Zone 2" of Ninja Foodi 2-Basket Air Fryer with a piece of foil.
6. Press your chosen zone - "Zone 1" or "Zone 2" and then rotate the knob to select "Air Fry".
7. Set the heat to 180 degrees C and then set the time for 5 minutes to preheat.
8. After preheating, arrange salmon fillets into the basket of each zone.
9. Brush with honey and sprinkle with chili flakes and sesame seeds.
10. Slide the basket into the Air Fryer and set the time for 12 minutes.
11. After cooking time is completed, remove the salmon fillets from Air Fryer and serve hot.

Serving Suggestions: Serve with lemon wedges.
Variation Tip: Use maple syrup for sweet taste.

Ingredients:

2 salmon fillets
¾ teaspoon toasted sesame oil
1 teaspoon sesame seeds
½ tablespoon low-sodium soy sauce
½ tablespoon honey
¼ teaspoon crushed chili flakes
Salt and pepper, to taste

Nutritional Information per Serving: Calories: 335 | Fat: 16.6g | Sat Fat: 2.8g | Carbohydrates: 18.3g | Fibre: 1g | Sugar: 14.1g | Protein: 29.8g

Healthy Fried Salmon with Asparagus

⏰ **Prep: 10 minutes**   🍲 **Cook: 3 minutes**   🍽 **Serves: 4**

Preparation:

1. In a small dish, mix lemon juice, olive oil, salt, pepper, dill and parsley.
2. Add salmon fillets in the mixture, coat well and set aside.
3. Now, add asparagus in the dill mixture and mix well.
4. Grease basket of Ninja Foodi 2-Basket Air Fryer.
5. Press your chosen zone - "Zone 1" or "Zone 2" and then rotate the knob to select "Air Fry".
6. Set the heat to 200 degrees C and then set the time for 5 minutes to preheat.
7. After preheating, arrange asparagus into the basket of each zone.
8. Slide the basket into the Air Fryer and set the time for 13 minutes.
9. After 3 minutes of cooking, arrange 2 salmon fillets on top of asparagus in each basket.
10. After cooking time is completed, remove the salmon fillets and asparagus from Air Fryer and serve hot.

Serving Suggestions: Serve with lemon wedges on the top.
Variation Tip: Don't use skinless salmon fillets.

Ingredients:

3 tablespoons lemon juice
4 tablespoons fresh dill, roughly chopped
4 salmon fillets
2 tablespoons olive oil
4 tablespoons fresh parsley, roughly chopped
900g asparagus
Salt and pepper, to taste

Nutritional Information per Serving: Calories: 296 | Fat: 14.3g | Sat Fat: 2g | Carbohydrates: 6.1g | Fibre: 0.3g | Sugar: 5.7g | Protein: 37g

Homemade Breaded Tilapia Fillets

Preparation: minutes   🍲 **Cook: 2 minutes**   🍽 **Serves: 6**

1. In a shallow dish, beat eggs and add cayenne pepper, plain flour, salt and pepper in it. Mix well.
2. Add breadcrumbs in another bowl and set aside.
3. Dip the tilapia fillets into egg mixture and then coat with the breadcrumbs mixture.
4. Grease basket of Ninja Foodi 2-Basket Air Fryer.
5. Press your chosen zone - "Zone 1" or "Zone 2" and then rotate the knob to select "Air Fry".
6. Set the heat to 180 degrees C and then set the time for 5 minutes to preheat.
7. After preheating, arrange tilapia fillets into the basket of each zone.
8. Slide the basket into the Air Fryer and set the time for 12 minutes.
9. While cooking, flip the tilapia fillets once halfway through.
10. After cooking time is completed, remove the tilapia fillets and from Air Fryer and serve hot.

Serving Suggestions: Serve with hot sauce.
Variation Tip: You can use oregano to enhance taste.

Ingredients:

4 large eggs
½ teaspoon cayenne pepper powder
4 large tilapia fillets, patted dry
6 tablespoons plain flour
300g breadcrumbs
Salt and pepper, to taste

Nutritional Information per Serving: Calories: 352 | Fat: 6.9g | Sat Fat: 2g | Carbohydrates: 45.3g | Fibre: 2.7g | Sugar: 3.6g | Protein: 26.2g

Crispy Cajun Cod Fillets

⏰ **Prep: 15 minutes**   🍲 **Cook: 6 minutes**   📚 **Serves: 6**

Preparation:

1. Add almond flour, smoked paprika, gluten-free flour, garlic powder, salt, Cajun seasoning, and pepper in a shallow dish. Whisk well.
2. Coat the fillets with flour mixture and refrigerate for about 2 hours.
3. Grease basket of Ninja Foodi 2-Basket Air Fryer.
4. Press your chosen zone – "Zone 1" or "Zone 2" and then rotate the knob to select "Air Fry".
5. Set the temperature to 200 degrees C and then set the time for 5 minutes to preheat.
6. After preheating, arrange the cod fillets into the basket of each zone.
7. Slide the basket into the Air Fryer and set the time for 16 minutes.
8. While cooking, flip the cod fillets once halfway through.
9. After cooking time is completed, remove the cod fillets from Air Fryer and serve hot.

Serving Suggestions: Serve with hot sauce.
Variation Tip: Regular flour can be used instead of gluten-free flour.

Ingredients:

6 cod fillets
3 tablespoons almond flour
1 teaspoon smoked paprika
30g gluten-free flour
2 teaspoons Cajun seasoning
½ teaspoon garlic powder
Salt and pepper, to taste

Nutritional Information per Serving: Calories: 139 | Fat: 1.1g | Sat Fat: 0.2g | Carbohydrates: 4.4g | Fibre: 0.7g | Sugar: 0.2g | Protein: 26.3g

Fresh Garlic Butter Prawns with Parsley

⏰ **Prep: 15 minutes**   🍲 **Cook: minutes**   📚 **Serves: 6**

Preparation:

1. Add butter, parsley, olive oil, minced garlic, salt and pepper in a large bowl. Whisk well.
2. Add in prawns in the mixture and toss to coat well.
3. Press "Zone 1" and "Zone 2" of Ninja Foodi 2-Basket Air Fryer and then rotate the knob for each zone to select "Bake".
4. Set the temperature to 230 degrees C and then set the time for 5 minutes to preheat.
5. After preheating, arrange 1 pan into the basket of each zone.
6. Slide the basket into the Air Fryer and set the time for 8 minutes.
7. After cooking time is completed, remove the pans from Air Fryer and serve hot.

Serving Suggestions: Serve with the garnishing of fresh herbs.
Variation Tip: Frozen prawns can also be used.

Ingredients:

900g fresh prawns
175g unsalted butter, melted
6 tablespoons fresh parsley, chopped
4 tablespoons olive oil
4 teaspoons minced garlic
Salt and pepper, to taste

Nutritional Information per Serving: Calories: 350 | Fat: 26.2g | Sat Fat: 12.5g | Carbohydrates: 2.4g | Fibre: 0.1g | Sugar: 0g | Protein: 26.2g

Air Fried Salmon Fillets

⏰ **Prep: 10 minutes**   🍲 **Cook: 0 minutes**   📚 **Serves: 4**

Preparation:

1. Grease basket of Ninja Foodi 2-Basket Air Fryer.
2. Press your chosen zone - "Zone 1" or "Zone 2" and then rotate the knob to select "Air Fry".
3. Set the temperature to 180 degrees C and then set the time for 5 minutes to preheat.
4. Season each salmon fillet with salt and black pepper and then coat with the oil.
5. After preheating, arrange salmon fillets in the basket of each zone.
6. Slide the basket into the Air Fryer and set the time for 10 minutes.
7. After cooking time is completed, remove the salmon fillets from Air Fryer and serve hot.

Serving Suggestions: Serve with the garnishing of spring onion.
Variation Tip: Use skinless salmon fillets.

Ingredients:

4 (150g) salmon fillets
Salt and ground black pepper, as required
2 tablespoons olive oil

Nutritional Information per Serving: Calories: 285 | Fat: 17.5g | Sat Fat: 2.5g | Carbohydrates: 0g | Fibre: 0g | Sugar: 0g | Protein: 33g

Lemon-Chili Salmon

⏰ **Prep: 10 minutes**   🍲 **Cook: minutes**   📚 **Serves: 4**

Preparation:

1. Grease basket of Ninja Foodi 2-Basket Air Fryer.
2. Press your chosen zone - "Zone 1" or "Zone 2" and then rotate the knob to select "Air Fry".
3. Set the temperature to 190 degrees C and then set the time for 5 minutes to preheat.
4. Season the salmon fillets with chili powder, salt, and black pepper evenly.
5. After preheating, arrange salmon fillets in the basket of each zone.
6. Arrange lemon slices over each salmon fillet.
7. Slide the basket into the Air Fryer and set the time for 8 minutes.
8. After cooking time is completed, remove the salmon fillets from Air Fryer and serve hot.

Serving Suggestions: Serve alongside the steamed green beans.
Variation Tip: Be sure that salmon should look bright and shiny before buying.

Ingredients:

4 (150g) salmon fillets
½ teaspoon red chili powder
Salt and ground black pepper, as required
1 lemon, cut into slices

Nutritional Information per Serving: Calories: 16 | Fat: 0g | Sat Fat: 0g | Carbohydrates: 2.1g | Fibre: 0.1g | Sugar: 0.7g | Protein: 0.2g

Tasty Sweet & Sour Salmon

⏰ **Prep:** 10 minutes 🍲 **Cook:** 2 minutes 📚 **Serves:** 4

Preparation:

1. In a small bowl, mix together the soy sauce, maple syrup, lemon juice and water.
2. Reserve about half of the mixture in another small bowl.
3. Add salmon fillets in the remaining mixture and coat well.
4. Cover the bowl and refrigerate to marinate for about 2 hours.
5. Remove the salmon fillets from refrigerator and shake off the excess marinade.
6. Line each basket of "Zone 1" and "Zone 2" of Ninja Foodi 2-Basket Air Fryer with a piece of foil.
7. Press your chosen zone - "Zone 1" or "Zone 2" and then rotate the knob to select "Air Fry".
8. Set the temperature to 180 degrees C and then set the time for 5 minutes to preheat.
9. After preheating, arrange salmon fillets in the basket of each zone.
10. Slide the basket into the Air Fryer and set the time for 12 minutes.
11. After cooking time is completed, remove the salmon fillets from Air Fryer. Serve hot.

Serving Suggestions: Garnish with sesame seeds.
Variation Tip: Use freshly squeezed lemon juice.

Ingredients:

180ml soy sauce
180g maple syrup
6 teaspoons fresh lemon juice
2 teaspoons water
8 (90g) salmon fillets

Nutritional Information per Serving: Calories: 335 | Fat: 16.6g | Sat Fat: 2.8g | Carbohydrates: 18.3g | Fibre: 1g | Sugar: 14.1g | Protein: 29.8g

Lemony Herbed Salmon with Asparagus

⏰ **Prep:** 15 minutes 🍲 **Cook:** 1 minutes 📚 **Serves:** 4

Preparation:

1. In a small bowl, mix together the lemon juice, oil, herbs, salt, and black pepper.
2. In a large bowl, mix together the salmon and ¾ of oil mixture.
3. In a second large bowl, add the asparagus and remaining oil mixture and mix well.
4. Grease basket of Ninja Foodi 2-Basket Air Fryer.
5. Press your chosen zone - "Zone 1" or "Zone 2" and then rotate the knob to select "Air Fry".
6. Set the temperature to 200 degrees C and then set the time for 5 minutes to preheat.
7. After preheating, arrange asparagus into the basket of each zone.
8. Slide the basket into the Air Fryer and set the time for 11 minutes.
9. After 3 minutes of cooking, arrange salmon fillets on top of asparagus in each basket.
10. After cooking time is completed, remove the salmon fillets and asparagus from Air Fryer and serve hot.

Serving Suggestions: Serve alongside the lemon slices.
Variation Tip: Don't use frozen salmon fillets.

Ingredients:

4 (150g) boneless salmon fillets
3 tablespoons fresh lemon juice
2 tablespoons olive oil
4 tablespoons fresh parsley, roughly chopped
4 tablespoons fresh dill, roughly chopped
400g asparagus
Salt and ground black pepper, as required

Nutritional Information per Serving: Calories: 320 | Fat: 17.9g | Sat Fat: 2.7g | Carbohydrates: 6.6g | Fibre: 3g | Sugar: 2.4g | Protein: 36.3g

Chapter 5 Poultry Mains Recipes

Garlicky Cumin Chicken Thighs

⏱ **Prep: 10 minutes**   🍲 **Cook: 20 minutes**   📚 **Serves: 4**

Preparation:

1. In a large bowl, add the spices, salt and black pepper and mix well.
2. Coat the chicken thighs with oil and then rub with spice mixture.
3. Grease basket of Ninja Foodi 2-Basket Air Fryer.
4. Press your chosen zone - "Zone 1" or "Zone 2" and then rotate the knob to select "Air Fry".
5. Set the temperature to 200 degrees C and then set the time for 5 minutes to preheat.
6. After preheating, arrange the chicken thighs into the basket of each zone.
7. Slide the basket into the Air Fryer and set the time for 20 minutes.
8. While cooking, flip the chicken thighs once halfway through.
9. After cooking time is completed, remove the chicken thighs from Air Fryer and serve hot.

Serving Suggestions: Serve with fresh greens.
Variation Tip: Don't use chicken thighs with a faded colour.

Ingredients:

4 (60g) chicken thighs
1 teaspoon ground cumin
1 teaspoon garlic powder
1 tablespoon olive oil
½ teaspoon smoked paprika
½ teaspoon ground coriander
Salt and ground black pepper, as required

Nutritional Information per Serving: Calories: 601 | Fat: 25.7g | Sat Fat: 6.6g | Carbohydrates: 0.9g | Fibre: 0.2g | Sugar: 0.2g | Protein: 86.4g

Crunchy Breaded Chicken Breasts

⏱ **Prep: 15 minutes**   🍲 **Cook: 40 minutes**   📚 **Serves: 3**

Preparation:

1. In a shallow, dish place the flour.
2. In a second shallows dish, mix together the egg and coriander.
3. In a third shallow dish, place croutons.
4. Coat the chicken breasts with flour, then dip into eggs and finally coat with croutons.
5. Grease basket of Ninja Foodi 2-Basket Air Fryer.
6. Press your chosen zone - "Zone 1" or "Zone 2" and then rotate the knob to select "Bake".
7. Set the temperature to 190 degrees C and then set the time for 5 minutes to preheat.
8. After preheating, arrange the chicken breasts into the basket of each zone.
9. Slide the basket into the Air Fryer and set the time for 40 minutes.
10. While cooking, flip the chicken breasts once halfway through.
11. After cooking time is completed, remove the chicken breasts from Air Fryer
12. Serve hot.

Serving Suggestions: Serve with tomato ketchup.
Variation Tip: Coat the chicken breasts evenly.

Ingredients:

3 (60g) boneless, skinless chicken breasts
5g fresh coriander, chopped
40g croutons, crushed
30g flour
1 large egg, beaten

Nutritional Information per Serving: Calories: 668 | Fat: 24.5g | Sat Fat: 6.8g | Carbohydrates: 15.5g | Fibre: 0.8g | Sugar: 0.2g | Protein: 90.5g

Crispy Cheese Chicken Tenderloins

🕐 **Prep: 8 minutes** 🍲 **Cook: 15 minutes** 🍽 **Serves: 4**

Preparation:

1. Place breadcrumbs in a shallow dish and add panko, cheese and pepper flakes.
2. Take another shallow bowl, microwave butter until melted.
3. Sprinkle chicken with salt.
4. Dip chicken in butter, then coat with crumb mixture.
5. Grease basket of Ninja Foodi 2-Basket Air Fryer.
6. Press your chosen zone - "Zone 1" or "Zone 2" and then rotate the knob to select "Air Fry".
7. Set the heat to 200 degrees C and then set the time for 5 minutes to preheat.
8. After preheating, arrange chicken strips into the basket of each zone.
9. Slide the basket into the Air Fryer and set the time for 7 minutes.
10. While cooking, flip the chicken once halfway through.
11. After cooking time is completed, remove the chicken from Air Fryer and serve hot.

Serving Suggestions: Serve with mashed potatoes.
Variation Tip: You can adjust the amount of spices according to your taste.

Ingredients:

455g chicken tenderloins
¼ teaspoon crushed red pepper flakes
½ teaspoon salt
50g grated Parmesan cheese
50g panko breadcrumbs
60g butter, cubed

Nutritional Information per Serving: Calories: 259 | Fat: 13.8g | Sat Fat: 8.2g | Carbohydrates: 2.3g | Fibre: 0.1g | Sugar: 0.1g | Protein: 24.5g

Baked Turkey Breast

🕐 **Prep: 10 minutes** 🍲 **Cook: 1 hour 20 minutes** 🍽 **Serves: 6**

Preparation:

1. Rub the turkey breast with the salt and black pepper evenly.
2. Grease basket of Ninja Foodi 2-Basket Air Fryer.
3. Press your chosen zone - "Zone 1" or "Zone 2" and then rotate the knob to select "Bake".
4. Set the temperature to 200 degrees C and then set the time for 5 minutes to preheat.
5. After preheating, arrange the turkey breast into the basket of each zone.
6. Slide the basket into the Air Fryer and set the time for 80 minutes.
7. After cooking time is completed, remove the turkey breasts from Air Fryer and place onto a platter.
8. With a piece of foil, cover each turkey breast for about 20 minutes before slicing.
9. With a sharp knife, cut each turkey breast into desired size slices and serve.

Serving Suggestions: Serve alongside roasted veggies.
Variation Tip: Avoid using turkey breast with flat spots.

Ingredients:

1 bone-in, skin-on turkey breast half
Salt and ground black pepper, as required

Nutritional Information per Serving: Calories: 40 | Fat: 0.6g | Sat Fat: 0.1g | Carbohydrates: 5.7g | Fibre: 0.3g | Sugar: 0.5g | Protein: 2.8g

Chapter 5 Poultry Mains Recipes

Air Fryer Spiced Duck Legs

⏰ **Prep:** 10 minutes 🍲 **Cook:** 30 minutes 📚 **Serves:** 2

Preparation:

1. In a bowl, add the garlic, parsley, five-spice powder, salt and black pepper and mix until well combined.
2. Rub the duck legs with garlic mixture generously.
3. Grease basket of Ninja Foodi 2-Basket Air Fryer.
4. Press your chosen zone - "Zone 1" or "Zone 2" and then rotate the knob to select "Air Fry".
5. Set the temperature to 170 degrees C and then set the time for 5 minutes to preheat.
6. After preheating, arrange the duck legs into the basket of each zone.
7. Slide the basket into the Air Fryer and set the time for 30 minutes.
8. After cooking time is completed, remove the duck legs from Air Fryer and serve hot.

Serving Suggestions: Serve alongside the fresh salad.
Variation Tip: Make sure that the skin of duck legs is clear and soft.

Ingredients:
2 duck legs
2 tablespoons fresh parsley, chopped
2 teaspoons five-spice powder
2 garlic cloves, minced
Salt and ground black pepper, as required

Nutritional Information per Serving: Calories: 188 | Fat: 4.5g | Sat Fat: 1g | Carbohydrates: 4.3g | Fibre: 6.6g | Sugar: 0.1g | Protein: 25.5g

Beer-Marinated Duck Breast

⏰ **Prep:** 10 minutes 🍲 **Cook:** 15 minutes 📚 **Serves:** 2

Preparation:

1. In a bowl, place the beer, oil, mustard, thyme, salt, and black pepper and mix well.
2. Add the duck breasts and coat with marinade generously.
3. Cover and refrigerate for about 4 hours.
4. Remove from the refrigerator and with a piece of foil, cover each duck breast.
5. Press "Zone 1" of Ninja Foodi 2-Basket Air Fryer and then rotate the knob for each zone to select "Air Fry".
6. Set the temperature to 200 degrees C and then set the time for 5 minutes to preheat.
7. After preheating, arrange the duck breast into the basket of each zone.
8. Slide the basket into the Air Fryer and set the time for 15 minutes.
9. After 5 minutes of cooking, remove the foil from duck breast and set the temperature to 180 degrees C.
10. After cooking time is completed, remove the duck breast from Air Fryer.
11. Place the duck breasts onto a cutting board for about 5 minutes before slicing.
12. With a sharp knife, cut each duck breast into desired size slices and serve.

Serving Suggestions: Serve alongside the cranberry sauce.
Variation Tip: You can use oil of your choice.

Ingredients:
1 duck breast
1 teaspoon mustard
1 tablespoon fresh thyme, chopped
240ml beer
1 tablespoon olive oil
Salt and ground black pepper, as required

Nutritional Information per Serving: Calories: 226 | Fat: 10.8g | Sat Fat: 1.1g | Carbohydrates: 5.7g | Fibre: 0.7g | Sugar: 0.1g | Protein: 18.7g

Crispy Chicken Tenders

⏰ **Prep:** 5 minutes   🍲 **Cook:** 10 minutes   📚 **Serves:** 2

Preparation:

1. Cut chicken breasts into thin 2.5 cm strips.
2. Set up the batter by putting flour and eggs in two separate bowls. Whisk the eggs.
3. In a large bowl, mix together panko breadcrumbs, garlic powder, onion powder, paprika, Italian seasoning and salt and pepper.
4. Dip chicken breasts into flour, then the eggs, and then finally breadcrumbs.
5. Grease basket of Ninja Foodi 2-Basket Air Fryer.
6. Press your chosen zone - "Zone 1" or "Zone 2" and then rotate the knob to select "Air Fry".
7. Set temperature to 200 degrees C and then set the time for 5 minutes to preheat.
8. After preheating, arrange coated chicken into the basket of each zone.
9. Slide the basket into the Air Fryer and set the time for 7-10 minutes.
10. After cooking time is completed, remove from Air Fryer.
11. Cut each portion into half and serve hot.

Serving Suggestions: Serve with your favourite fresh salad.
Variation Tip: You can add fresh herbs.

Ingredients:

225g chicken breasts
30g flour
1 egg
⅛ teaspoon paprika
¼ teaspoon onion powder
¼ teaspoon garlic powder
¼ teaspoon Italian seasoning
25g panko breadcrumbs
Salt and pepper, to taste

Nutritional Information per Serving: Calories: 308 | Fat: 10.9g | Sat Fat: 3g | Carbohydrates: 12.8g | Fibre: 0.5g | Sugar: 0.5g | Protein: 37.3

Crunchy Breaded Chicken Cutlets

⏰ **Prep:** 8 minutes   🍲 **Cook:** 10 minutes   📚 **Serves:** 2

Preparation:

1. Rub the chicken with salt and pepper.
2. In a bowl, whisk the eggs.
3. Take another bowl and combine the breadcrumbs and seasoning.
4. Dip chicken cutlet in the eggs and then lay it in breadcrumbs. Do this on the either sides of the chicken cutlet.
5. Grease basket of Ninja Foodi 2-Basket Air Fryer.
6. Press your chosen zone - "Zone 1" or "Zone 2" and then rotate the knob to select "Air Fry".
7. Set temperature to 200 degrees C and then set the time for 5 minutes to preheat.
8. After preheating, arrange 1 chicken cutlet into the basket of each zone.
9. Slide the basket into the Air Fryer and set the time for 10 to 12 minutes.
10. After cooking time is completed, remove the chicken cutlets from Air Fryer and place each onto a platter for about 10 minutes before serving.
11. Serve and enjoy.

Serving Suggestions: Serve with steamed veggies.
Variation Tip: Fresh chicken should have a pinkish colour.

Ingredients:

2 chicken cutlets
25g Italian breadcrumbs
1 egg
¼ teaspoon paprika
⅛ teaspoon garlic powder
⅛ teaspoon onion powder
Salt and pepper, to taste

Nutritional Information per Serving: Calories: 353 | Fat: 13.3g | Sat Fat: 3.7g | Carbohydrates: 10.3g | Fibre: 0.8g | Sugar: 1.1g | Protein: 45.2g

Buttery Chicken Breast

⏰ Prep: 2 minutes 🍲 Cook: 10 minutes 🗂 Serves: 2

Preparation:

1. Melt butter and add in garlic powder, salt and pepper. Combine well.
2. Take a cutting board and place chicken breasts.
3. Coat chicken with butter mixture.
4. Grease basket of Ninja Foodi 2-Basket Air Fryer.
5. Press your chosen zone - "Zone 1" or "Zone 2" and then rotate the knob to select "Air Fry".
6. Set the heat to 195 degrees C and then set the time for 5 minutes to preheat.
7. After preheating, arrange chicken breasts into the basket of each zone.
8. Slide the basket into the Air Fryer and set the time for 10 to 15 minutes.
9. After cooking time is completed, remove the chicken breasts from Air Fryer and serve hot.

Serving Suggestions: Serve alongside the orange slices.
Variation Tip: You can adjust the amount of spices according to your taste.

Ingredients:

2 boneless chicken breasts
⅛ teaspoon pepper
1 tablespoon butter
¼ teaspoon salt
⅛ teaspoon garlic powder

Nutritional Information per Serving: Calories: 318 | Fat: 16.1g | Sat Fat: 6.5g | Carbohydrates: 0.2g | Fibre: 0.1g | Sugar: 0g | Protein: 40.6g

Spicy Chicken Wings

⏰ Prep: 10 minutes 🍲 Cook: 35 minutes 🗂 Serves: 3

Preparation:

1. In a large bowl, combine garlic powder, mustard, ginger, nutmeg, garlic salt, allspice, baking soda, pepper and cayenne pepper.
2. Cut chicken wings into sections.
3. Add to the bowl and stir firmly to coat.
4. Grease basket of Ninja Foodi 2-Basket Air Fryer.
5. Press your chosen zone - "Zone 1" or "Zone 2" and then rotate the knob to select "Air Fry".
6. Set the heat to 150 degrees C and then set the time for 5 minutes to preheat.
7. After preheating, arrange chicken wings into the basket of each zone.
8. Slide the basket into the Air Fryer and set the time for 30 to 35 minutes.
9. After cooking time is completed, remove the chicken legs from Air Fryer and serve hot.

Serving Suggestions: Serve with roasted veggies.
Variation Tip: You can add fresh herbs of your choice.

Ingredients:

455g whole chicken wings
1 teaspoon garlic powder
½ teaspoon garlic salt
¼ teaspoon cayenne pepper
¼ teaspoon baking soda
¼ teaspoon ground allspice
¼ teaspoon pepper
½ teaspoon mustard
½ teaspoon ginger
½ teaspoon nutmeg

Nutritional Information per Serving: Calories: 91 | Fat: 6.4g | Sat Fat: 1.9g | Carbohydrates: 0.4g | Fibre: 0.1g | Sugar: 0.1g | Protein: 8.1g

Almond Crusted Chicken

⏰ **Prep:** 15 minutes   🍲 **Cook:** 30 minutes   📚 **Serves:** 2

Preparation:

1. Take a shallow bowl, whisk egg, buttermilk, pepper and garlic salt.
2. Place almonds in another shallow bowl.
3. Dip chicken breasts into the egg mixture and then coat with almonds.
4. Grease basket of Ninja Foodi 2-Basket Air Fryer.
5. Press your chosen zone - "Zone 1" or "Zone 2" and then rotate the knob to select "Air Fry".
6. Set the temperature to 175 degrees C and then set the time for 5 minutes to preheat.
7. After preheating, arrange the chicken into the basket of each zone.
8. Slide the basket into the Air Fryer and set the time for 15 to 18 minutes.
9. After cooking time is completed, remove chicken from Air Fryer and serve hot.

Serving Suggestions: Serve with mashed potatoes.
Variation Tip: Fresh chicken should have a pinkish colour.

Ingredients:

2 chicken breast halves, boneless and skinless
2 small eggs
1 teaspoon garlic salt
4 tablespoons buttermilk
70g silvered almonds, finely chopped
½ teaspoon pepper

Nutritional Information per Serving: Calories: 466 | Fat: 29.2g | Sat Fat: 3.1g | Carbohydrates: 13.3g | Fibre: 6.2g | Sugar: 4.1g | Protein: 42g

Sweet Potato Chips-Crusted Chicken

⏰ **Prep:** 10 minutes   🍲 **Cook:** 10 minutes   📚 **Serves:** 2

Preparation:

1. In a food processor, add chips, pepper, salt and baking powder. Pulse until ground.
2. Transfer to a shallow bowl.
3. Take a bowl, mix cornflour and remaining salt.
4. Place the chicken in the cornflour mixture and then toss with potato chip mixture.
5. Grease basket of Ninja Foodi 2-Basket Air Fryer.
6. Press your chosen zone - "Zone 1" or "Zone 2" and then rotate the knob to select "Air Fry".
7. Set the temperature to 200 degrees C and then set the time for 5 minutes to preheat.
8. After preheating, arrange chicken nuggets into the basket of each zone.
9. Slide the basket into the Air Fryer and set the time for 10 minutes.
10. After cooking time is completed, remove the chicken nuggets from Air Fryer and serve hot.

Serving Suggestions: Serve with fresh salad.
Variation Tip: You can also use breadcrumbs.

Ingredients:

225g chicken tenderloins, cut into pieces
½ tablespoon cornflour
50g sweet potato chips
½ teaspoon salt, divided
2 tablespoons plain flour
¼ teaspoon coarsely ground pepper
⅛ teaspoon baking powder

Nutritional Information per Serving: Calories: 173 | Fat: 3.4g | Sat Fat: 0.3g | Carbohydrates: 11.6g | Fibre: 0.7g | Sugar: 0.8g | Protein: 24g

Crispy Herbed Chicken

⏰ **Prep:** 10 minutes   🍲 **Cook:** 20 minutes   📚 **Serves:** 6

Preparation:

1. Take a bowl, add all ingredients except chicken and egg. Mix well.
2. Take another bowl and whisk egg.
3. Dip chicken in egg, then coat with cracker mixture.
4. Grease basket of Ninja Foodi 2-Basket Air Fryer.
5. Press your chosen zone - "Zone 1" or "Zone 2" and then rotate the knob to select "Air Fry".
6. Set the heat to 190 degrees C and then set the time for 5 minutes to preheat.
7. After preheating, arrange chicken into the basket of each zone.
8. Slide the basket into the Air Fryer and set the time for 15 to 20 minutes.
9. After cooking time is completed, remove the chicken from Air Fryer and place onto a platter.
10. Serve and enjoy.

Serving Suggestions: Serve alongside the steamed veggies.
Variation Tip: You can adjust the amount of spices according to your taste.

Ingredients:

900g chicken, cut up
85g crushed Ritz crackers
½ teaspoon paprika
½ teaspoon garlic salt
½ tablespoon minced fresh parsley
⅛ teaspoon rubbed sage
⅛ teaspoon ground cumin
¼ teaspoon pepper
1 small egg, beaten

Nutritional Information per Serving: Calories: 518 | Fat: 12.5g | Sat Fat: 3g | Carbohydrates: 5.9g | Fibre: 0.3g | Sugar: 1.3g | Protein: 90g

---

Buttery Bagel Crusted Chicken Strips

⏰ **Prep:** 8 minutes   🍲 **Cook:** 15 minutes   📚 **Serves:** 2

Preparation:

1. Take a food processor, pulse torn bagel until crumbs are formed.
2. Place breadcrumbs in a shallow dish and add panko, cheese and pepper flakes.
3. Take another shallow bowl, microwave butter until melted.
4. Sprinkle chicken with salt.
5. Dip chicken in butter, then coat with crumb mixture.
6. Grease basket of Ninja Foodi 2-Basket Air Fryer.
7. Press your chosen zone - "Zone 1" or "Zone 2" and then rotate the knob to select "Air Fry".
8. Set the heat to 200 degrees C and then set the time for 5 minutes to preheat.
9. After preheating, arrange chicken tenderloins into the basket of each zone.
10. Slide the basket into the Air Fryer and set the time for 7 minutes.
11. While cooking, flip the chicken once halfway through.
12. After cooking time is completed, remove the chicken from Air Fryer and serve hot.

Serving Suggestions: Serve with buttery mashed potatoes.
Variation Tip: You can adjust the amount of spices according to your taste.

Ingredients:

225g chicken tenderloins
Bagel, torn
25g grated Parmesan cheese
25g panko breadcrumbs
30g butter, cubed
⅛ teaspoon crushed red pepper flakes
¼ teaspoon salt

Nutritional Information per Serving: Calories: 331 | Fat: 14.3g | Sat Fat: 8.3g | Carbohydrates: 16.6g | Fibre: 0.7g | Sugar: 1.5g | Protein: 27.4g

Chapter 5 Poultry Mains Recipes | 43

Lemony Cheese Chicken Breast

⏱ **Prep: 15 minutes** 🍲 **Cook: 25 minutes** 🍽 **Serves: 2**

Preparation:

1. Take a baking dish, place chicken and pour lemon juice over chicken.
2. Sprinkle with feta cheese, oregano and pepper.
3. Press "Zone 1" of Ninja Foodi 2-Basket Air Fryer and then rotate the knob for each zone to select "Air Fry".
4. Set the heat to 200 degrees C and then set the time for 5 minutes to preheat.
5. After preheating, arrange chicken into the basket of each zone.
6. Slide the basket into the Air Fryer and set the time for 20 to 25 minutes.
7. After cooking time is completed, remove the chicken breast from Air Fryer.
8. Serve and enjoy.

Serving Suggestions: Serve alongside lemon juice.
Variation Tip: Use cheese of your choice.

Ingredients:

2 chicken breast halves, boneless and skinless
2 tablespoons crumbled feta cheese
½ teaspoon dried oregano
¼ teaspoon pepper
2 tablespoons lemon juice

Nutritional Information per Serving: Calories: 296 | Fat: 12.5g | Sat Fat: 4.4g | Carbohydrates: 1.1g | Fibre: 0.3g | Sugar: 0.7g | Protein: 42g

Hot and Spicy Chicken Breasts

⏱ **Prep: 10 minutes** 🍲 **Cook: 16 minutes** 🍽 **Serves: 2**

Preparation:

1. In a bowl, whisk Greek yogurt, egg substitute and hot sauce.
2. Take another bowl, mix panko breadcrumbs, paprika, garlic pepper and cayenne pepper.
3. Dip chicken strips into yogurt mixture and then coat with panko breadcrumb mixture.
4. Grease basket of Ninja Foodi 2-Basket Air Fryer.
5. Press your chosen zone - "Zone 1" or "Zone 2" and then rotate the knob to select "Air Fry".
6. Set the temperature to 200 degrees C and then set the time for 5 minutes to preheat.
7. After preheating, arrange coated chicken into the basket of each zone.
8. Slide the basket into the Air Fryer and set the time for 8 minutes per side.
9. After cooking time is completed, remove the chicken strips from Air Fryer and serve hot.

Serving Suggestions: Serve alongside hot sauce.
Variation Tip: You can also use egg whites as a substitute.

Ingredients:

225g chicken breasts, skinless and boneless
½ tablespoon cayenne pepper
½ tablespoon garlic pepper seasoning
½ tablespoon sweet paprika
½ teaspoon hot sauce
55g panko breadcrumbs
2 tablespoons egg substitute
60g plain fat-free Greek yogurt

Nutritional Information per Serving: Calories: 272 | Fat: 6.4g | Sat Fat: 2.4g | Carbohydrates: 8.1g | Fibre: 1.3g | Sugar: 1.4g | Protein: 30g

Herbed Spicy Whole Chicken

⏱ **Prep:** 15 minutes 🍲 **Cook:** 1 hour 10 minutes
📚 **Serves:** 12

Preparation:

1. In a bowl, add the butter, herbs, spices and salt and mix well.
2. Rub each chicken with spice mixture generously.
3. With kitchen twine, tie off the wings and legs of each chicken.
4. Grease basket of Ninja Foodi 2-Basket Air Fryer.
5. Press your chosen zone - "Zone 1" or "Zone 2" and then rotate the knob to select "Bake".
6. Set the temperature to 180 degrees C and then set the time for 5 minutes to preheat.
7. After preheating, arrange 1 chicken into the basket of each zone.
8. Slide the basket into the Air Fryer and set the time for 70 minutes.
9. After cooking time is completed, remove the chickens from Air Fryer and place each onto a platter for about 10 minutes before serving.
10. Cut each chicken into desired-sized pieces and serve.

Serving Suggestions: Serve with steamed veggies.
Variation Tip: Fresh chicken should have a pinkish colour.

Ingredients:

115g butter, softened
4 teaspoons dried rosemary
4 teaspoons dried thyme
2 tablespoons Cajun seasoning
2 tablespoons onion powder
2 tablespoons garlic powder
2 tablespoons paprika
2 teaspoons cayenne pepper
Salt, as required
2 (1.4kg) whole chicken, neck and giblets removed

Nutritional Information per Serving: Calories: 421 | Fat: 14.8g | Sat Fat: 6.9g | Carbohydrates: 2.3g | Fibre: 0.9g | Sugar: 0.5g | Protein: 66.3g

Sour & Spicy Chicken Legs

⏱ **Prep:** 15 minutes 🍲 **Cook:** 20 minutes 📚 **Serves:** 4

Preparation:

1. In a bowl, add the chicken legs, vinegar, garlic and salt and mix well.
2. Set aside for about 15 minutes.
3. Meanwhile, in another bowl, mix together the yogurt, spices, salt and black pepper.
4. Add the chicken legs into the bowl and coat with the spice mixture generously.
5. Cover the bowl of chicken and refrigerate for at least 10-12 hours.
6. Grease basket of Ninja Foodi 2-Basket Air Fryer.
7. Press your chosen zone - "Zone 1" or "Zone 2" and then rotate the knob to select "Air Fry".
8. Set the temperature to 200 degrees C and then set the time for 5 minutes to preheat.
9. After preheating, arrange 2 chicken legs into the basket of each zone.
10. Slide the basket into the Air Fryer and set the time for 20 minutes.
11. After cooking time is completed, remove the chicken legs from Air Fryer and serve hot.

Serving Suggestions: Serve alongside the orange slices.
Variation Tip: You can adjust the ratio of spices according to your taste.

Ingredients:

4 (200g) chicken legs
2 tablespoons balsamic vinegar
2 teaspoons garlic, minced
Salt, as required
4 tablespoons plain Greek yogurt
1 teaspoon red chili powder
1 teaspoon ground cumin
1 teaspoon ground coriander
Ground black pepper, as required

Nutritional Information per Serving: Calories: 450 | Fat: 17.2g | Sat Fat: 4.8g | Carbohydrates: 2.2g | Fibre: 0.3g | Sugar: 1.2g | Protein: 66.7g

Crispy Paprika Chicken Legs

⏰ **Prep: 15 minutes** 🍲 **Cook: 20 minutes** 📚 **Serves: 6**

Preparation:

1. In a shallow bowl, place the milk.
2. In another shallow bowl, mix together the flour and spices.
3. Dip the chicken legs into milk and then coat with the flour mixture.
4. Repeat this process once again.
5. Grease basket of Ninja Foodi 2-Basket Air Fryer.
6. Press your chosen zone - "Zone 1" or "Zone 2" and then rotate the knob to select "Air Fry".
7. Set the temperature to 180 degrees C and then set the time for 5 minutes to preheat.
8. After preheating, arrange chicken legs in the basket of each zone.
9. Slide the basket into the Air Fryer and set the time for 25 minutes.
10. After cooking time is completed, remove the chicken legs from Air Fryer and serve hot.

Serving Suggestions: Serve with roasted veggies.
Variation Tip: Select chicken legs with a pinkish hue.

Ingredients:

480ml milk
250g flour
2 teaspoons garlic powder
2 teaspoons onion powder
2 teaspoons ground cumin
2 teaspoons paprika
Salt and ground black pepper, as required
6 (200g) chicken legs

Nutritional Information per Serving: Calories: 372| Fat: 12.9g | Sat Fat: 3.9g | Carbohydrates: 15.5g | Fibre: 0.8g | Sugar: 0.2g | Protein: 45.4g

Gingered Chicken Drumsticks

⏰ **Prep: 10 minutes** 🍲 **Cook: 25 minutes** 📚 **Serves: 6**

Preparation:

1. In a large bowl, place the coconut milk, galangal, ginger, and spices and mix well.
2. Add the chicken drumsticks and coat with the marinade generously.
3. Refrigerate to marinate for at least 6-8 hours.
4. Grease basket of Ninja Foodi 2-Basket Air Fryer.
5. Press your chosen zone - "Zone 1" or "Zone 2" and then rotate the knob to select "Air Fry".
6. Set the temperature to 190 degrees C and then set the time for 5 minutes to preheat.
7. After preheating, arrange 3 drumsticks into the basket of each zone.
8. Slide the basket into the Air Fryer and set the time for 25 minutes.
9. After cooking time is completed, remove the drumsticks from Air Fryer and serve hot.

Serving Suggestions: Serve with your favourite vegetables.
Variation Tip: You can use grated fresh turmeric.

Ingredients:

120ml full-fat coconut milk
4 teaspoons fresh ginger, minced
4 teaspoons galangal, minced
2 teaspoons ground turmeric
Salt, as required
6 (150g) chicken drumsticks

Nutritional Information per Serving: Calories: 347 | Fat: 14.8g | Sat Fat: 6.9g | Carbohydrates: 3.8g | Fibre: 1.1g | Sugar: 0.8g | Protein: 47.6g

Honey & Mustard Chicken Drumsticks

⏱ Prep: 10 minutes 🍲 Cook: 20 minutes ≋ Serves: 4

Preparation:

1. In a bowl, add all ingredients except the drumsticks and mix until well combined.
2. Add the drumsticks and coat with the mixture generously.
3. Cover the bowl and place in the refrigerator to marinate overnight.
4. Grease either basket of "Zone 1" or "Zone 2" of Ninja Foodi 2-Basket Air Fryer.
5. Press your chosen zone - "Zone 1" or "Zone 2" and then rotate the knob to select "Air Fry".
6. Set the temperature to 160 degrees C and then set the time for 5 minutes to preheat.
7. After preheating, arrange drumsticks into the basket.
8. Slide basket into Air Fryer and set the time for 12 minutes.
9. After 12 minutes, flip the drumsticks and set the temperature to 200 degrees C.
10. Set the time for 8 minutes.
11. After cooking time is completed, remove the drumsticks from Air Fryer and serve hot.

Serving Suggestions: Serve with the drizzling of lime juice.
Variation Tip: You can use fresh herbs of your choice.

Ingredients:

60g Dijon mustard
1 tablespoon honey
2 tablespoons rapeseed oil
1 tablespoon fresh parsley, minced
Salt and ground black pepper, as required
4 (150g) chicken drumsticks

Nutritional Information per Serving: Calories: 376 | Fat: 17.4g | Sat Fat: 3.1g | Carbohydrates: 5.2g | Fibre: 0.6g | Sugar: 4.5g | Protein: 47.5g

Parmesan Chicken Breasts

⏱ Prep: 15 minutes 🍲 Cook: 22 minutes ≋ Serves: 4

Preparation:

1. In a shallow bowl, beat the egg.
2. In a separate bowl, add the breadcrumbs, oil, and basil and mix until a crumbly mixture forms.
3. Now, dip each chicken breast into the beaten egg and then coat with the breadcrumb mixture.
4. Grease basket of Ninja Foodi 2-Basket Air Fryer.
5. Press your chosen zone - "Zone 1" or "Zone 2" and then rotate the knob to select "Air Fry".
6. Set the temperature to 175 degrees C and then set the time for 5 minutes to preheat.
7. After preheating, arrange 2 chicken breasts into the basket of each zone.
8. Slide the basket into the Air Fryer and set the time for 22 minutes.
9. After 15 minutes of cooking, spoon the pasta sauce over each chicken breast, followed by the cheese.
10. After cooking time is completed, remove the chicken breasts from Air Fryer and serve hot.

Serving Suggestions: Serve with your favourite fresh salad.
Variation Tip: You can replace pasta sauce with tomato sauce too.

Ingredients:

4 (150g) chicken breasts
2 eggs, beaten
200g breadcrumbs
2 tablespoons fresh basil
4 tablespoons olive oil
120g pasta sauce
50g Parmesan cheese, grated

Nutritional Information per Serving: Calories: 768 | Fat: 35.4g | Sat Fat: 8.8g | Carbohydrates: 457g | Fibre: 3.4g | Sugar: 6.5g | Protein: 63.9g

Chapter 5 Poultry Mains Recipes

Cheese & Spinach Stuffed Chicken Breasts

⏰ **Prep: 15 minutes**   🍲 **Cook: 30 minutes**   📚 **Serves: 4**

Preparation:

1. In a medium frying pan, heat the oil over medium heat and cook the spinach for about 3-4 minutes.
2. Stir in the ricotta and cook for about 40-60 seconds.
3. Remove the frying pan from heat and set aside to cool.
4. Cut slits into the chicken breasts about ½ cm apart but not all the way through.
5. Stuff each chicken breast with the spinach mixture.
6. Season each chicken breast with salt and black pepper and then sprinkle the top with Parmesan cheese and paprika.
7. Grease basket of Ninja Foodi 2-Basket Air Fryer.
8. Press your chosen zone - "Zone 1" or "Zone 2" and then rotate the knob to select "Air Fry".
9. Set the temperature to 200 degrees C and then set the time for 5 minutes to preheat.
10. After preheating, arrange 2 chicken breasts into the basket of each zone.
11. Slide the basket into the Air Fryer and set the time for 25 minutes.
12. After cooking time is completed, remove the chicken breasts from Air Fryer and serve hot.

Serving Suggestions: Serve with fresh salad.
Variation Tip: You can use kale instead of spinach.

Ingredients:

2 tablespoon olive oil
85g fresh spinach
125g ricotta cheese, shredded
4 (100g) skinless, boneless chicken breasts
Salt and ground black pepper, as required
4 tablespoons Parmesan cheese, grated
½ teaspoon paprika

Nutritional Information per Serving: Calories: 272 | Fat: 15g | Sat Fat: 5g | Carbohydrates: 2.8g | Fibre: 0.7g | Sugar: 0.2g | Protein: 31.5g

---

Easy Baked Turkey Breast

⏰ **Prep: 10 minutes**   🍲 **Cook: 1 hour 20 minutes**   📚 **Serves: 12**

Preparation:

1. Rub the turkey breast with the salt and black pepper evenly.
2. Grease basket of Ninja Foodi 2-Basket Air Fryer.
3. Press your chosen zone - "Zone 1" or "Zone 2" and then rotate the knob to select "Bake".
4. Set the temperature to 200 degrees C and then set the time for 5 minutes to preheat.
5. After preheating, arrange 1 turkey breast into the basket of each zone.
6. Slide the basket into the Air Fryer and set the time for 80 minutes.
7. After cooking time is completed, remove the turkey breasts from Air Fryer and place onto a platter.
8. With a piece of foil, cover each turkey breast for about 20 minutes before slicing.
9. With a sharp knife, cut each turkey breast into desired size slices and serve.

Serving Suggestions: Serve alongside the steamed veggies.
Variation Tip: Avoid using turkey breast with flat spots.

Ingredients:

2 (1.2kg) bone-in, skin-on turkey breast half
Salt and ground black pepper, as required

Nutritional Information per Serving: Calories: 326 | Fat: 14.6g | Sat Fat: 4g | Carbohydrates: 0g | Fibre: 0g | Sugar: 0g | Protein: 45.6g

Chapter 6 Beef, Pork & Lamb Recipes

Easy Air Fried Lamb Steak

⏰ **Prep: 2 minutes** 🍲 **Cook: 7 minutes** 🍽 **Serves: 2**

Preparation:

1. Take a bowl, add every ingredient except lamb steak. Mix well.
2. Rub lamb steaks with a little olive oil.
3. Press each side of steak into salt and pepper mixture.
4. Grease basket of Ninja Foodi 2-Basket Air Fryer.
5. Press your chosen zone - "Zone 1" or "Zone 2" and then rotate the knob to select "Air Fry".
6. Set the heat to 200 degrees C and then set the time for 5 minutes to preheat.
7. After preheating, arrange steak into the basket of each zone.
8. Slide the basket into the Air Fryer and set the time for 5 minutes.
9. While cooking, flip the steak once halfway through and cook for more 5 minutes.
10. After cooking time is completed, remove it from the Air Fryer and place in a platter for about 10 minutes before slicing.
11. With a sharp knife, cut each steak into desired-sized slices and serve.

Serving Suggestions: Serve with mashed potatoes.
Variation Tip: Feel free to use the seasoning of your choice.

Ingredients:

2 lamb steaks
½ teaspoon salt
Drizzle of olive oil
½ teaspoon ground black pepper

Nutritional Information per Serving: Calories: 190 | Fat: 7.4g | Sat Fat: 2.4g | Carbohydrates: 3.7g | Fibre: 1.5g | Sugar: 2.6g | Protein: 24.8g

Tasty Beef Roast

⏰ **Prep: 10 minutes** 🍲 **Cook: 50 minutes** 🍽 **Serves: 8**

Preparation:

1. Grease either basket "Zone 1" or "Zone 2" of Ninja Foodi 2-Basket Air Fryer.
2. Press your chosen zone - "Zone 1" or "Zone 2" and then rotate the knob for the zone to select "Roast".
3. Set the temperature to 175 degrees C and then set the time for 5 minutes to preheat.
4. Rub roast with salt and black pepper generously.
5. After preheating, arrange the roast into the basket.
6. Slide basket into Air Fryer and set the time for 50 minutes.
7. After cooking time is completed, remove roast from Air Fryer and place onto a platter for about 10 minutes before slicing.
8. With a sharp knife, cut roast into desired-sized slices and serve.

Serving Suggestions: Serve with lemon wedges.
Variation Tip: Feel free to use the seasoning of your choice.

Ingredients:

1 (455g) beef roast
Salt and ground black pepper, as required

Nutritional Information per Serving: Calories: 105 | Fat: 3.5g | Sat Fat: 1.3g | Carbohydrates: 0g | Fibre: 0g | Sugar: 0g | Protein: 17.2g

BBQ Honey Pork Ribs

⏰ **Prep: 15 minutes** 🍲 **Cook: 26 minutes** 📚 **Serves: 4**

Preparation:

1. In a bowl, mix together honey and the remaining ingredients except pork ribs.
2. Add the pork ribs and coat with the mixture generously.
3. Refrigerate to marinate for about 20 minutes.
4. Grease basket of Ninja Foodi 2-Basket Air Fryer.
5. Press your chosen zone - "Zone 1" or "Zone 2" and then rotate the knob to select "Air Fry".
6. Set the temperature to 180 degrees C and then set the time for 5 minutes to preheat.
7. After preheating, arrange the ribs into the basket of each zone.
8. Slide the basket into the Air Fryer and set the time for 26 minutes.
9. While cooking, flip the ribs once halfway through.
10. After cooking time is completed, remove the ribs from Air Fryer and place onto serving plates.
11. Drizzle with the remaining honey and serve immediately.

Serving Suggestions: Serve with steamed veggies.
Variation Tip: You can use BBQ sauce of your choice.

Ingredients:

900g pork ribs
85g honey, divided
240g BBQ sauce
½ teaspoon garlic powder
2 tablespoons tomato ketchup
1 tablespoon Worcestershire sauce
1 tablespoon low-sodium soy sauce
Freshly ground white pepper, as required

Nutritional Information per Serving: Calories: 791 | Fat: 40.4g | Sat Fat: 14.3g | Carbohydrates: 43.3g | Fibre: 0.5g | Sugar: 36.5g | Protein: 60.6g

Simple Air Fried New York Strip Steak

⏰ **Prep: 10 minutes** 🍲 **Cook: 10 minutes** 📚 **Serves: 2**

Preparation:

1. Grease either basket of "Zone 1" and "Zone 2" in Ninja Foodi 2-Basket Air Fryer.
2. Press your chosen zone - "Zone 1" or "Zone 2" and then rotate the knob for each zone to select "Air Fry".
3. Set the temperature to 200 degrees C for the zone and then set the time for 5 minutes to preheat.
4. Coat the steaks with oil and then sprinkle with salt and black pepper evenly.
5. After preheating, arrange the steak into the basket.
6. Slide basket into Air Fryer and set the time for 10 minutes.
7. While cooking, flip the steak once halfway through.
8. After cooking time is completed, remove the steak from Air Fryer and place onto a platter for about 10 minutes.
9. Cut steak into desired size slices and serve immediately.

Serving Suggestions: Serve with fresh baby kale.
Variation Tip: Season the steaks with salt and black pepper generously.

Ingredients:

1 (110g) New York strip steaks
1½ teaspoons olive oil
Salt and ground black pepper, as required

Nutritional Information per Serving: Calories: 809 | Fat: 56.3g | Sat Fat: 18.9g | Carbohydrates: 0g | Fibre: 0g | Sugar: 0g | Protein: 77.7g

Chapter 6 Beef, Pork & Lamb Recipes

Air Fryer Bacon Wrapped Hot Dogs

⏱ **Prep: 10 minutes** 🍲 **Cook: 15 minutes** ≋ **Serves: 2**

Preparation:

1. Wrap each hot dog with bacon strip and season with salt and black pepper.
2. Grease basket of Ninja Foodi 2-Basket Air Fryer.
3. Press your chosen zone - "Zone 1" or "Zone 2" and then rotate the knob to select "Air Fry".
4. Set the temperature to 200 degrees C and then set the time for 5 minutes to preheat.
5. After preheating, arrange bacon wrapped hot dogs into the basket of each zone.
6. Slide the basket into the Air Fryer and set the time for 15 minutes.
7. While cooking, flip the hot dogs once halfway through.
8. After cooking time is completed, remove the filets from Air Fryer and serve hot.

Serving Suggestions: Serve alongside the green beans.
Variation Tip: Black pepper can be replaced with cayenne pepper.

Ingredients:

2 bacon strips
2 hot dogs
Salt and black pepper, to taste

Nutritional Information per Serving: Calories: 242 | Fat: 21.7g | Sat Fat: 8g | Carbohydrates: 1.8g | Fibre: 0g | Sugar: 1.5g | Protein: 8.8g

Herbed Garlic Pork Chops

⏱ **Prep: 15 minutes** 🍲 **Cook: 12 minutes** ≋ **Serves: 2**

Preparation:

1. In a bowl, mix together the garlic, herbs, oil, mustard, coriander, sugar, and salt.
2. Add the pork chops and coat with marinade generously.
3. Cover and refrigerate for about 2-3 hours.
4. Remove the chops from the refrigerator. Set aside at room temperature for about 30 minutes before cooking.
5. Grease either basket of "Zone 1" or "Zone 2" of Ninja Foodi 2-Basket Air Fryer.
6. Press your chosen zone - "Zone 1" or "Zone 2" and then rotate the knob for each zone to select "Air Fry".
7. Set the temperature to 200 degrees C for the zone and then set the time for 5 minutes to preheat.
8. After preheating, arrange pork chops into the basket.
9. Slide basket into Air Fryer and set the time for 12 minutes.
10. After cooking time is completed, remove the chops from Air Fryer.
11. Serve hot.

Serving Suggestions: Serve with your favourite dipping sauce.
Variation Tip: Look for chops that are pinkish-red in colour.

Ingredients:

2 (75g) (2.5cm thick) pork chops
2 tablespoons olive oil
1 tablespoon Dijon mustard
½ tablespoon ground coriander
1 teaspoon sugar
2 garlic cloves, minced
½ tablespoon fresh coriander, chopped
½ tablespoon fresh rosemary, chopped
½ tablespoon fresh parsley, chopped
Salt, as required

Nutritional Information per Serving: Calories: 413 | Fat: 35.6g | Sat Fat: 10g | Carbohydrates: 4g | Fibre: 0.7g | Sugar: 2.1g | Protein: 19.7g

Aromatic Cinnamon Lamb Meatballs

⏱ **Prep: 10 minutes**   🍲 **Cook: 12 minutes**   ≋ **Serves: 4**

Preparation:

1. Add lamb mince, onion, cinnamon, cumin, parsley, salt and pepper in a large bowl. Mix until well combined.
2. Make 2.5cm balls from the mixture and set aside.
3. Grease basket of Ninja Foodi 2-Basket Air Fryer.
4. Press your chosen zone - "Zone 1" or "Zone 2" and then rotate the knob to select "Air Fry".
5. Set the temperature to 195 degrees C and then set the time for 5 minutes to preheat.
6. After preheating, arrange the meatballs into the basket of each zone.
7. Slide the basket into the Air Fryer and set the time for 12 minutes.
8. Flip the meatballs once halfway through.
9. Take out and serve warm.

Serving Suggestions: Serve with the garnishing of sesame seeds.
Variation Tip: Strictly follow the ratio of ingredients.

Ingredients:

455g lamb mince
1 teaspoon ground cinnamon
1 teaspoon ground cumin
2 teaspoons granulated onion
2 tablespoons fresh parsley
Salt and black pepper, to taste

Nutritional Information per Serving: Calories: 215 | Fat: 8.5g | Sat Fat: 3g | Carbohydrates: 0.8g | Fibre: 0.4g | Sugar: 0g | Protein: 32g

Chili-Garlic Lamb Loin Chops

⏱ **Prep: 10 minutes**   🍲 **Cook: 13 minutes**   ≋ **Serves: 2**

Preparation:

1. In a large bowl, place all ingredients and mix well.
2. Refrigerate to marinate overnight.
3. Remove chops from bowl and season with a little salt.
4. Grease either basket of "Zone 1" or "Zone 2" of Ninja Foodi 2-Basket Air Fryer.
5. Press your chosen zone - "Zone 1" or "Zone 2" and then rotate the knob for the zone to select "Bake".
6. Set the temperature to 200 degrees C and then set the time for 5 minutes to preheat.
7. Rub the lamb chops with salt and black pepper generously.
8. After preheating, arrange lamb chops into the basket.
9. Slide basket into Air Fryer and set the time for 11 minutes.
10. Flip the chops once halfway through.
11. After cooking time is completed, remove the chops from Air Fryer and serve hot.

Serving Suggestions: Serve with the drizzling of lemon juice.
Variation Tip: Don't undercook the lamb chops.

Ingredients:

4 (50g, 1 cm thick) lamb loin chops
2 garlic cloves, crushed
1 teaspoon chili powder
2 teaspoons fresh rosemary, minced
Salt and ground black pepper, as required

Nutritional Information per Serving: Calories: 223 | Fat: 8.7g | Sat Fat: 3.1g | Carbohydrates: 2.5g | Fibre: 1g | Sugar: 0.1g | Protein: 32.3g

Cajun Flank Steak

⏰ **Prep: 10 minutes** 🍲 **Cook: 7 minutes** ≋ **Serves: 4**

Preparation:

1. Grease either basket of "Zone 1" or "Zone 2" of Ninja Foodi 2-Basket Air Fryer.
2. Press your chosen zone - "Zone 1" or "Zone 2" and then rotate the knob for the zone to select "Bake".
3. Set the temperature to 215 degrees C and then set the time for 5 minutes to preheat.
4. Rub the steaks with Cajun seasoning evenly.
5. After preheating, arrange steak into the basket.
6. Slide basket into Air Fryer and set the time for 7 minutes.
7. After cooking time is completed, remove the steak from Air Fryer and set aside to cool.
8. Slice and serve.

Serving Suggestions: Serve with fresh baby greens.
Variation Tip: Taco seasoning can also be used.

Ingredients:

900g flank steak
1 Cajun seasoning
½ teaspoon smoked paprika
Salt, to taste

Nutritional Information per Serving: Calories: 441 | Fat: 18.9g | Sat Fat: 7.8g | Carbohydrates: 0.1g | Fibre: 0.1g | Sugar: 0g | Protein: 63.1g

Herbed Garlic Lamb Chops

⏰ **Prep: 5 minutes** 🍲 **Cook: 10 minutes** ≋ **Serves: 2**

Preparation:

1. Take a bowl, add oil, thyme, garlic, salt, pepper and rosemary. Mix well.
2. Add in lamb chops and toss to coat well.
3. Continue until we have a chops well coated with seasonings.
4. Grease either basket of "Zone 1" or "Zone 2" of Ninja Foodi 2-Basket Air Fryer.
5. Press your chosen zone - "Zone 1" or "Zone 2" and then rotate the knob for the zone to select "Bake".
6. Set the heat to 195 degrees C and then set the time for 5 minutes to preheat.
7. After preheating, arrange lamb chops into the basket.
8. Slide basket into Air Fryer and set the time for 10 to 15 minutes.
9. While cooking, flip the lamb chops once halfway through.
10. After cooking time is completed, remove the lamb chops from Air Fryer and serve hot.

Serving Suggestions: Serve alongside the greens.
Variation Tip: Thickness of chops may affect cooking time

Ingredients:

225g lamb, pre-cut chops
1 tablespoon olive oil
1 teaspoon fresh rosemary
½ teaspoon fresh minced garlic
¼ teaspoon salt
¼ teaspoon pepper
½ teaspoon thyme

Nutritional Information per Serving: Calories: 275 | Fat: 15.4g | Sat Fat: 4g | Carbohydrates: 0.9g | Fibre: 0.4g | Sugar: 0g | Protein: 32g

Baked Lamb Steaks

⏰ **Prep:** 2 minutes　🍲 **Cook:** 7 minutes　📚 **Serves:** 2

Preparation:

1. Take a bowl, add every ingredient except lamb steak. Mix well.
2. Rub lamb steaks with a little olive oil.
3. Press each side of steak into salt and pepper mixture.
4. Grease either basket of "Zone 1" or "Zone 2" of Ninja Foodi 2-Basket Air Fryer.
5. Press your chosen zone - "Zone 1" or "Zone 2" and then rotate the knob for the zone to select "Bake".
6. Set the heat to 200 degrees C and then set the time for 5 minutes to preheat.
7. After preheating, arrange steak into the basket.
8. Slide basket into Air Fryer and set the time for 5 minutes.
9. While cooking, flip the steak once halfway through and cook for more 5 minutes.
10. After cooking time is completed, remove it from Air Fryer and place onto a platter for about 10 minutes before slicing.
11. With a sharp knife, cut steak into desired-sized slices and serve.

Serving Suggestions: Serve with lemon wedges.
Variation Tip: Feel free to use the seasoning of your choice.

Ingredients:

2 lamb steaks
½ teaspoon salt
½ teaspoon ground black pepper
Drizzle of olive oil

Nutritional Information per Serving: Calories: 159 | Fat: 6.3g | Sat Fat: 2.2g | Carbohydrates: 0.3g | Fibre: 0.1g | Sugar: 0g | Protein: 23.9g

Herbed Beef Roast with Onion

⏰ **Prep:** 15 minutes　🍲 **Cook:** 35 minutes　📚 **Serves:** 3

Preparation:

1. Grease either basket of "Zone 1" or "Zone 2" of Ninja Foodi 2-Basket Air Fryer.
2. Press your chosen zone - "Zone 1" or "Zone 2" and then rotate the knob for the zone to select "Bake".
3. Set the temperature to 175 degrees C and then set the time for 5 minutes to preheat.
4. Add salt, rosemary, thyme and olive oil in a bowl. Mix well.
5. Rub the mixture on the roast and set aside.
6. After preheating, place onion and arrange roast into the basket.
7. Slide basket into Air Fryer and set the time for 35 minutes.
8. After cooking time is completed, remove roast from Air Fryer and place onto a platter.
9. Slice and serve.

Serving Suggestions: Serve with melted butter on the top.
Variation Tip: Fresh rosemary can also be used.

Ingredients:

455g beef roast
½ onion, chopped
1 teaspoon dried rosemary
1 teaspoon dried thyme
½ tablespoon olive oil
Salt, to taste

Nutritional Information per Serving: Calories: 310 | Fat: 11.9g | Sat Fat: 3.9g | Carbohydrates: 2.2g | Fibre: 0.7g | Sugar: 0.8g | Protein: 46.1g

Chapter 6 Beef, Pork & Lamb Recipes

Homemade BBQ Baby Back Ribs

⏰ **Prep: 10 minutes** 🍳 **Cook: 30 minutes** 📚 **Serves: 6**

Preparation:

1. In a bowl, mix together BBQ sauce, BBQ rub and water.
2. Add the pork ribs and coat with the mixture generously.
3. Refrigerate to marinate for about 20 minutes.
4. Grease basket of Ninja Foodi 2-Basket Air Fryer.
5. Press your chosen zone - "Zone 1" or "Zone 2" and then rotate the knob to select "Air Fry".
6. Set the temperature to 180 degrees C and then set the time for 5 minutes to preheat.
7. After preheating, arrange the ribs into the basket of each zone.
8. Slide the basket into the Air Fryer and set the time for 30 minutes.
9. While cooking, flip the ribs once halfway through.
10. After cooking time is completed, remove the ribs from Air Fryer and place onto serving plates.
11. Serve and enjoy!

Serving Suggestions: Serve with honey on the top.
Variation Tip: You can use BBQ sauce of your choice.

Ingredients:

1 rack baby back ribs
240g BBQ sauce
90g BBQ rub
240ml water

Nutritional Information per Serving: Calories: 177 | Fat: 6.1g | Sat Fat: 2.1g | Carbohydrates: 13.7g | Fibre: 0.4g | Sugar: 7.4g | Protein: 26g

Herbs Baked Pork Chops

⏰ **Prep: 10 minutes** 🍳 **Cook: 8 minutes** 📚 **Serves: 4**

Preparation:

1. Add parsley, thyme, paprika, basil, oregano, salt and olive oil in a large bowl. Mix well.
2. Add pork chops in the bowl and coat with marinade generously.
3. Cover and refrigerate for about 2-3 hours.
4. Remove the chops from the refrigerator and set aside at room temperature for about 30 minutes before cooking.
5. Grease either basket of "Zone 1" or "Zone 2" of Ninja Foodi 2-Basket Air Fryer.
6. Press your chosen zone - "Zone 1" or "Zone 2" and then rotate the knob for the zone to select "Bake".
7. Set the heat to 200 degrees C and then set the time for 5 minutes to preheat.
8. After preheating, arrange 4 chops into the basket.
9. Slide basket into Air Fryer and set the time for 8 minutes.
10. After cooking time is completed, remove the chops from Air Fryer.
11. Serve hot.

Serving Suggestions: Serve with your chopped mint leaves on the top.
Variation Tip: Coconut oil can also be used instead of olive oil.

Ingredients:

4 pork chops
2 tablespoons parsley
2 tablespoons thyme
4 tablespoons paprika
2 tablespoons basil
2 tablespoons oregano
2 tablespoons olive oil
Salt, to taste

Nutritional Information per Serving: Calories: 348 | Fat: 28.1g | Sat Fat: 8.7g | Carbohydrates: 6.3g | Fibre: 4.1g | Sugar: 0.8g | Protein: 19.5g

Chapter 6 Beef, Pork & Lamb Recipes

Delicious Bacon Wrapped Pork Tenderloin

⏱ **Prep: 15 minutes** 🍲 **Cook: 20 minutes** 📚 **Serves: 12**

Preparation:

1. Season pork tenderloins with salt and pepper and set aside.
2. Wrap pork tenderloin with bacon strips and set aside for a while.
3. Grease basket of Ninja Foodi 2-Basket Air Fryer.
4. Press your chosen zone - "Zone 1" or "Zone 2" and then rotate the knob to select "Air Fry".
5. Set the heat to 180 degrees C and then set the time for 5 minutes to preheat.
6. After preheating, arrange bacon wrapped pork tenderloins into the basket of each zone.
7. Slide the basket into the Air Fryer and set the time for 20 minutes.
8. After cooking time is completed, remove bacon wrapped pork tenderloins from Air Fryer and place on a plate.
9. Slice and serve.

Serving Suggestions: Serve with fresh parsley on the top.
Variation Tip: Chili flakes can be used for spicy taste.

Ingredients:

2 (900g) pork tenderloins
12 bacon strips
½ teaspoon ground black pepper
Salt, to taste

Nutritional Information per Serving: Calories: 556 | Fat: 27.4g | Sat Fat: 9.7g | Carbohydrates: 0.1g | Fibre: 0.1g | Sugar: 0g | Protein: 71.7g

Simple Taco Seasoned Lamb Chops

⏱ **Prep: 10 minutes** 🍲 **Cook: 10 minutes** 📚 **Serves: 2**

Preparation:

1. Grease either basket of "Zone 1" or "Zone 2" of Ninja Foodi 2-Basket Air Fryer.
2. Press your chosen zone - "Zone 1" or "Zone 2" and then rotate the knob for the zone to select "Bake".
3. Set the temperature to 190 degrees C and then set the time for 5 minutes to preheat.
4. Rub the lamb chops generously with salt, black pepper and taco seasoning.
5. After preheating, arrange lamb chop into the basket.
6. Slide basket into Air Fryer and set the time for 10 minutes.
7. After cooking time is completed, remove the chops from Air Fryer and serve hot.

Serving Suggestions: Serve with chopped mint leaves.
Variation Tip: Lemon juice can also be added to enhance taste.

Ingredients:

2 lamb chops
2 tablespoons taco seasoning
Salt and pepper, to taste

Nutritional Information per Serving: Calories: 729 | Fat: 37.8g | Sat Fat: 19.7g | Carbohydrates: 41.1g | Fibre: 0g | Sugar: 0g | Protein: 55.7g

Rosemary Garlic Lamb Chops

🕐 **Prep: 10 minutes**   🍲 **Cook: 14 minutes**   ≋ **Serves: 8**

Preparation:

1. Add rosemary, salt, black pepper, garlic powder and olive oil in a large bowl. Mix well.
2. Add in lamb chops and toss to coat well.
3. Cover them and set aside for an hour.
4. Grease basket of Ninja Foodi 2-Basket Air Fryer.
5. Press your chosen zone - "Zone 1" or "Zone 2" and then rotate the knob to select "Bake".
6. Set the temperature to 200 degrees C and then set the time for 5 minutes to preheat.
7. After preheating, arrange the lamb chops into the basket of each zone.
8. Slide the basket into the Air Fryer and set the time for 14 minutes.
9. Flip the chops once halfway through.
10. After cooking time is completed, remove the chops from Air Fryer and serve hot.

Serving Suggestions: Serve with the drizzling of lemon juice.
Variation Tip: Avocado oil can also be used.

Ingredients:

1.1kg lamb chops
4 tablespoons fresh rosemary, chopped
6 tablespoons olive oil
2 teaspoons garlic powder
Salt and black pepper, to taste

Nutritional Information per Serving: Calories: 1205 | Fat: 54.4g | Sat Fat: 17.2g | Carbohydrates: 1.6g | Fibre: 0.8g | Sugar: 0.2g | Protein: 167.4g

Easy Beef Sirloin Roast

🕐 **Prep: 10 minutes**   🍲 **Cook: 50 minutes**   ≋ **Serves: 16**

Preparation:

1. Grease basket of Ninja Foodi 2-Basket Air Fryer.
2. Press your chosen zone - "Zone 1" or "Zone 2" and then rotate the knob to select "Roast".
3. Set the temperature to 175 degrees C and then set the time for 5 minutes to preheat.
4. Rub the roast with salt and black pepper generously.
5. After preheating, arrange 1 roast into the basket of each zone.
6. Slide the basket into the Air Fryer and set the time for 50 minutes.
7. After cooking time is completed, remove each roast from Air Fryer and place onto a platter for about 10 minutes before slicing.
8. With a sharp knife, cut each roast into desired-sized slices and serve.

Serving Suggestions: Serve with lemon wedges.
Variation Tip: Feel free to use the seasoning of your choice.

Ingredients:

2 (1.1kg) sirloin roast
Salt and ground black pepper, as required

Nutritional Information per Serving: Calories: 281| Fat: 111.7g | Sat Fat: 4.2g | Carbohydrates: 0g | Fibre: 0g | Sugar: 0g | Protein: 40.9g

Chapter 6 Beef, Pork & Lamb Recipes

Chapter 7 Dessert Recipes

Easy Butter Cake

⏰ Prep: 10 minutes 🍲 Cook: 15 minutes 📚 Serves: 6

Preparation:

1. In a bowl, add the butter and sugar. Whisk until creamy.
2. Now, add the egg and whisk until fluffy.
3. Add the flour and salt. Mix well with the milk.
4. Place the mixture evenly into the greased cake pan.
5. Press either "Zone 1" or "Zone 2" and then rotate the knob for the zone to select "Air Fry".
6. Set the temperature to 175 degrees C and then set the time for 5 minutes to preheat.
7. After preheating, arrange the pan into the basket.
8. Slide basket into Air Fryer and set the time for 15 minutes.
9. After cooking time is completed, remove the pan from Air Fryer.
10. Set aside to cool.
11. Serve and enjoy!

Serving Suggestions: Serve with icing sugar.
Variation Tip: Refrigerate before serving.

Ingredients:
1 egg
3 tablespoons butter, softened
120ml milk
1 tablespoon icing sugar
100g caster sugar
185g plain flour
A pinch of salt

Nutritional Information per Serving: Calories: 253 | Fat: 7.2g | Sat Fat: 4.2g | Carbohydrates: 42.9g | Fibre: 0.8g | Sugar: 19g | Protein: 4.9g

Apple Crumble

⏰ Prep: 5 minutes 🍲 Cook: 25 minutes 📚 Serves: 4

Preparation:

1. Take a baking dish.
2. Arrange apple pie filling evenly into the prepared baking dish.
3. Take a large bowl, add all the remaining ingredients. Mix well.
4. Place the mixture evenly all over apple pie filling.
5. Press either "Zone 1" or "Zone 2" and then rotate the knob to select "Bake".
6. Set the temperature to 160 degrees C and then set the time for 5 minutes to preheat.
7. After preheating, arrange the baking dish into the basket.
8. Slide basket into Air Fryer and set the time for 25 minutes.
9. After cooking time is completed, remove the baking dish from Air Fryer.
10. Set aside to cool.
11. Serve and enjoy!

Serving Suggestions: Serve with icing sugar.
Variation Tip: Refrigerate before using.

Ingredients:
1 can apple pie filling
6 tablespoons caster sugar
8 tablespoons self-rising flour
60g butter, softened
A pinch of salt

Nutritional Information per Serving: Calories: 380 | Fat: 11.8g | Sat Fat: 7.3g | Carbohydrates: 70.2g | Fibre: 2g | Sugar: 39.3g | Protein: 1.9g

Raisins & Walnuts Semolina Cake

🕐 **Prep: 10 minutes** 🍲 **Cook: 15 minutes** 📚 **Serves: 6**

Preparation:

1. Take a bowl, add the semolina, oil, milk, sugar and yogurt. Mix well.
2. Cover the bowl and set aside for 15 minutes.
3. Add salt, baking soda and baking powder in the semolina mixture. Mix well.
4. Fold in the raisins and walnuts.
5. Press either "Zone 1" or "Zone 2" and then rotate the knob to select "Air Fry".
6. Set the temperature to 160 degrees C and then set the time for 5 minutes to preheat.
7. After preheating, arrange the pan into the basket.
8. Slide basket into Air Fryer and set the time for 15 minutes.
9. After cooking time is completed, remove the pan from Air Fryer.
10. Set aside to cool.
11. Serve and enjoy!

Serving Suggestions: Garnish with icing sugar.
Variation Tip: Refrigerate before serving.

Ingredients:

335g semolina
40g raisins
40g walnuts, chopped
½ teaspoon baking soda
1½ teaspoon baking powder
120ml vegetable oil
240ml milk
240g plain Greek yogurt
200g sugar
A pinch of salt

Nutritional Information per Serving: Calories: 536 | Fat: 21.9g | Sat Fat: 3.8g | Carbohydrates: 79.2g | Fibre: 2.7g | Sugar: 37g | Protein: 8.5g

Lemon Cheesecake

🕐 **Prep: 8 minutes** 🍲 **Cook: 25 minutes** 📚 **Serves: 2**

Preparation:

1. Press either "Zone 1" or "Zone 2" and then rotate the knob to select "Bake".
2. Set the temperature to 160 degrees C and then set the time for 5 minutes to preheat.
3. Take a bowl, mix together all the ingredients.
4. Place the mixture into a baking dish.
5. After preheating, arrange baking dish into the basket.
6. Slide basket into Air Fryer and set the time for 25 minutes.
7. After cooking time is completed, remove from the Air Fryer.
8. Set aside to cool.
9. Serve and enjoy!

Serving Suggestions: Garnish with icing sugar.
Variation Tip: Refrigerate before using.

Ingredients:

615g ricotta cheese
2 eggs
1 tablespoon fresh lemon juice
3 tablespoons corn flour
2 teaspoon vanilla extract
1 teaspoon fresh lemon zest, finely grated

Nutritional Information per Serving: Calories: 558 | Fat: 29g | Sat Fat: 16.7g | Carbohydrates: 30.7g | Fibre: 0.1g | Sugar: 2.1g | Protein: 40.9g

Vanilla Chocolate Cake

⏰ **Prep: 12 minutes** 🍲 **Cook: 25 minutes** 📚 **Serves: 6**

Preparation:

1. Take a bowl, add the flour, cocoa powder, baking powder, baking soda and salt. Mix well.
2. Now, add remaining ingredients and whisk well with an electric beater.
3. Place the mixture evenly into a greased cake pan.
4. Press either "Zone 1" and "Zone 2" and then rotate the knob to select "Air Fry".
5. Set the temperature to 160 degrees C and then set the time for 5 minutes to preheat.
6. After preheating, arrange the pan into the basket.
7. Slide basket into Air Fryer and set the time for 25 minutes.
8. After cooking time is completed, remove the pan from Air Fryer.
9. Set aside to cool.
10. Serve and enjoy!

Serving Suggestions: Serve with chocolate chips on top.
Variation Tip: Refrigerate before serving.

Ingredients:

3 eggs
120g sour cream
115g butter, softened
2 teaspoon vanilla extract
10 tablespoons sugar
125g flour
1 teaspoon baking powder
5 tablespoons cocoa powder
½ teaspoon baking soda
A pinch of salt

Nutritional Information per Serving: Calories: 374 | Fat: 22.4g | Sat Fat: 13.3g | Carbohydrates: 39.9g | Fibre: 1.9g | Sugar: 20.5g | Protein: 6.5g

Butter Oats Cookies

⏰ **Prep: 10 minutes** 🍲 **Cook: 7 minutes** 📚 **Serves: 20**

Preparation:

1. In a mixing dish, combine both sugars and melted butter. Blend until everything is well combined.
2. Combine the eggs and vanilla extract in a mixing bowl. Beat the drums thoroughly.
3. Sift the flour, baking soda, cinnamon, and salt over the top and whisk until everything is thoroughly combined.
4. Add the rolled oats and mix well.
5. Line the baskets of your Air Fryer with parchment paper.
6. Press your chosen zone - "Zone 1" or "Zone 2" and then rotate the knob to select "Air Fryer".
7. Set the temperature to 150 degrees C, and then set the time for 5 minutes to preheat.
8. After preheating, fill the Air Fryer basket with walnut-sized cookie dough balls of each zone.
9. Slide the baskets into Air Fryer and set the time for 7 minutes.
10. After cooking time is completed, transfer onto serving plates and serve.

Serving Suggestions: Top with chocolate syrup.
Variation Tip: You can skip the cinnamon.

Ingredients:

200g brown sugar
100g granulated sugar
230g butter, melted
2 large eggs
2 teaspoons vanilla extract
125g plain flour
1 teaspoon baking soda
1 teaspoon cinnamon
¾ teaspoon salt
250g rolled oats

Nutritional Information per Serving: Calories: 132 | Fat: 7g | Sat Fat: 4g | Carbohydrates: 2g | Fibre: 2g | Sugar: 9g | Protein: 4g

Best Churros

⏰ **Prep: 10 minutes**　🍲 **Cook: 13 minutes**　📚 **Serves: 8**

Preparation:

1. Bring the water, butter, sugar, and a pinch of salt to a boil in a medium saucepan over medium heat.
2. Reduce the heat to low and quickly stir in the flour with a wooden spatula after the mixture has reached a boil. Stir the mixture continuously until it thickens.
3. Mix everything in a stand mixer bowl.
4. Once the churros dough has cooled slightly, add the eggs one at a time, mixing constantly. Fill a piping bag with the churros mixture.
5. Pipe 7 – 10 cm long churros onto a baking sheet. Using a pair of scissors, cut the end. Freeze the baking sheet for at least 30 minutes.
6. Press your chosen zone - "Zone 1" or "Zone 2" and then rotate the knob to select "Air Fryer".
7. Set the temperature to 180 degrees C, and then set the time for 5 minutes to preheat.
8. After preheating, gently remove the frozen churros from the parchment paper. Then, place them into the air fryer basket of each zone.
9. Slide the baskets into Air Fryer and set the time for 7 minutes.
10. After cooking time is completed, transfer onto serving plates and serve.

Serving Suggestions: Serve with chocolate sauce.
Variation Tip: You can skip the cinnamon.

Ingredients:

180ml plus 2 tablespoons water
60g butter
1 tablespoon sugar
Pinch of salt
95g flour
2 medium eggs
100g sugar
1 teaspoon cinnamon

Nutritional Information per Serving: Calories: 60 | Fat: 3g | Sat Fat: 1g | Carbohydrates: 8g | Fibre: 1g | Sugar: 5g | Protein: 1g

Butter Brownies

⏰ **Prep: 20 minutes**　🍲 **Cook: 35 minutes**　📚 **Serves: 2**

Preparation:

1. Combine melted butter and sugar in a medium mixing bowl. Mix in the egg and vanilla extract thoroughly.
2. Stir in the dry ingredients until barely mixed.
3. Pour batter into the pans that have been prepared.
4. Press either "Zone 1" or "Zone 2" and then rotate the knob to select "Air Fryer".
5. Set the temperature to 165 degrees C, and then set the time for 5 minutes to preheat.
6. After preheating, place pans into the Air Fryer basket of chosen zone.
7. Slide the basket into the Air Fryer and set the time for 13 minutes.
8. After cooking time is completed, transfer onto serving plates and serve.

Serving Suggestions: Serve with vanilla ice cream.
Variation Tip: You can also add chopped pecans.

Ingredients:

60g butter, melted
100g sugar
1 egg
½ teaspoon vanilla extract
40g plain flour
3 tablespoons unsweetened cocoa
⅛ teaspoon baking powder
⅛ teaspoon salt

Nutritional Information per Serving: Calories: 520 | Fat: 26g | Sat Fat: 15g | Carbohydrates: 70g | Fibre: 3.3g | Sugar: 50g | Protein: 6g

Chapter 7 Dessert Recipes | 61

Lime Mousse

⏰ **Prep: 10 minutes**   🍲 **Cook: 12 minutes**   📚 **Serves: 4**

Preparation:

1. For mousse: Press either "Zone 1" or "Zone 2" and then rotate the knob to select "Bake".
2. Set the temperature to 175 degrees C and then set the time for 5 minutes to preheat.
3. In a bowl, add all the ingredients and mix until well combined.
4. Transfer the mixture into 4 ramekins.
5. After preheating, arrange ramekins into the basket.
6. Slide basket into Air Fryer and set the time for 12 minutes.
7. After cooking time is completed, remove the ramekins from Air Fryer.
8. Set the ramekins aside to cool.
9. Refrigerate the ramekins for at least 3 hours before serving.

Serving Suggestions: Serve with the topping of heavy whipping cream.
Variation Tip: You can replace lime with lemon.

Ingredients:

200g cream cheese, softened
240g heavy cream
4 tablespoons fresh lime juice
4 tablespoons maple syrup
Pinch of salt

Calories: 355 | Fat: 30.9g | Sat Fat: 19.4g | Carbohydrates: 15.9g | Fibre: 0g | Sugar: 12g | Protein: 4.9g

Chocolate Pistachios Muffins

⏰ **Prep: 15 minutes**   🍲 **Cook: 15 minutes**   📚 **Serves: 12**

Preparation:

1. In a bowl, add the flour, cocoa powder, baking powder, baking soda, and salt and mix well.
2. In another bowl, add the coconut milk, sugar, coconut oil and vanilla extract and beat until well combined.
3. Add the flour mixture and mix until just combined.
4. Fold in the chocolate chips and pistachios.
5. Grease 2 (6-cups) silicone muffin tins.
6. Place the mixture into prepared muffin cups about ¾ full.
7. Press your chosen zone - "Zone 1" or "Zone 2" and then rotate the knob to select "Air Fry".
8. Set the temperature to 150 degrees C and then set the time for 5 minutes to preheat.
9. After preheating, arrange 1 muffin tin into the basket of each zone.
10. Slide the basket into the Air Fryer and set the time for 15 minutes.
11. After cooking time is completed, remove the muffin tin from Air Fryer.
12. Place the muffin molds onto a wire rack to cool for about 10 minutes.
13. Carefully invert the muffins onto the wire rack to completely cool before serving.

Serving Suggestions: Serve with the sprinkling of sugar.
Variation Tip: Use best quality cocoa powder.

Ingredients:

1 250g plain flour
4 tablespoons cocoa powder
½ teaspoon baking soda
2 teaspoons baking powder
½ teaspoon salt
240ml coconut milk
100g granulated sugar
6 tablespoons coconut oil, melted
1 teaspoon vanilla extract
170g dark chocolate chips
60g pistachios, chopped

Nutritional Information per Serving: Calories: 278 | Fat: 15.9g | Sat Fat: 4.5g | Carbohydrates: 34.1g | Fibre: 4.6g | Sugar: 14.6g | Protein: 4.1g

Chocolate Chip Mug Cakes

⏱ **Prep: 15 minutes**   🍲 **Cook: 17 minutes**   ≋ **Serves: 4**

Preparation:

1. Press either "Zone 1" or "Zone 2" and then rotate the knob to select "Bake".
2. Set the temperature to 190 degrees C and then set the time for 5 minutes to preheat.
3. In a bowl, mix together the flour, sugar, baking soda, baking powder, and salt.
4. Add the milk, applesauce, oil and vanilla extract and mix until well combined.
5. Gently fold in the chocolate chips.
6. Divide the mixture into 4 heatproof mugs.
7. After preheating, arrange 2 mugs into the basket.
8. Slide basket into Air Fryer and set the time for 17 minutes.
9. After cooking time is completed, remove the mugs from Air Fryer.
10. Place the mugs onto a wire rack to cool for about 10 minutes before serving.

Serving Suggestions: Serve with the drizzling of chocolate sauce.
Variation Tip: Use best quality chocolate chips.

Ingredients:

125g flour
8 tablespoons sugar
1 teaspoon baking powder
½ teaspoon baking soda
¼ teaspoon salt
8 tablespoons milk
8 tablespoons applesauce
2 tablespoons vegetable oil
1 teaspoon vanilla extract
8 tablespoons chocolate chips

Nutritional Information per Serving: Calories: 409 | Fat: 14g | Sat Fat: 6.1g | Carbohydrates: 66g | Fibre: 2g | Sugar: 39.5g | Protein: 5.9g

Cherry Crumble

⏱ **Prep: 15 minutes**   🍲 **Cook: 25 minutes**   ≋ **Serves: 8**

Preparation:

1. In 2 lightly greased baking pans, place the cherry pie filling evenly.
2. In a medium bowl, combine the remaining ingredients and mix until a crumbly mixture forms.
3. Spread the mixture over cherry pie filling in each pan evenly.
4. Press your chosen zone - "Zone 1" or "Zone 2" and then rotate the knob to select "Air Fry".
5. Set the temperature to 160 degrees C and then set the time for 5 minutes to preheat.
6. After preheating, arrange 1 baking pan into the basket of each zone.
7. Slide the basket into the Air Fryer and set the time for 25 minutes.
8. After cooking time is completed, remove the baking pans from Air Fryer.
9. Place the baking pan onto a wire rack to cool for about 10 minutes before serving.

Serving Suggestions: Serve with the topping of whipped cream.
Variation Tip: use unsalted butter.

Ingredients:

2 (350g) cans cherry pie filling
115g butter, softened
125g plus 2 tablespoons self-rising flour
150g plus 2 tablespoons caster sugar
Pinch of salt

Nutritional Information per Serving: Calories: 334 | Fat: 11.8g | Sat Fat: 4.5g | Carbohydrates: 55.2g | Fibre: 1.1g | Sugar: 13.8g | Protein: 2.3g

Conclusion

With such advanced features, the Ninja Foodi Dual Air Fryer allows users to make the most of their time. Without having to stand over a pot stirring continuously or watching the barbeque grills for hours on end, users are free to do things that are more important. Whether it is finishing up work, spending time with your family, or simply relaxing, the Ninja Foodi Dual Air Fryer offers you the opportunity to do anything, while it takes care of cooking delicious dishes for you and your loved ones. If you have not gotten your hands on this must-have kitchen appliance already, you are missing out on so much. Grab one at the earliest and experience a new way of cooking that gets you excited to try new food every day.

Appendix 1 Measurement Conversion Chart

VOLUME EQUIVALENTS (LIQUID)

US STANDARD	US STANDARD (OUNCES)	METRIC (APPROXIMATE)
2 tablespoons	1 fl.oz	30 mL
¼ cup	2 fl.oz	60 mL
½ cup	4 fl.oz	120 mL
1 cup	8 fl.oz	240 mL
1½ cup	12 fl.oz	355 mL
2 cups or 1 pint	16 fl.oz	475 mL
4 cups or 1 quart	32 fl.oz	1 L
1 gallon	128 fl.oz	4 L

VOLUME EQUIVALENTS (DRY)

US STANDARD	METRIC (APPROXIMATE)
⅛ teaspoon	0.5 mL
¼ teaspoon	1 mL
½ teaspoon	2 mL
¾ teaspoon	4 mL
1 teaspoon	5 mL
1 tablespoon	15 mL
¼ cup	59 mL
½ cup	118 mL
¾ cup	177 mL
1 cup	235 mL
2 cups	475 mL
3 cups	700 mL
4 cups	1 L

TEMPERATURES EQUIVALENTS

FAHRENHEIT(F)	CELSIUS（C）(APPROXIMATE)
225 °F	107 °C
250 °F	120 °C
275 °F	135 °C
300 °F	150 °C
325 °F	160 °C
350 °F	180 °C
375 °F	190 °C
400 °F	205 °C
425 °F	220 °C
450 °F	235 °C
475 °F	245 °C
500 °F	260 °C

WEIGHT EQUIVALENTS

US STANDARD	METRIC (APPROXINATE)
1 ounce	28 g
2 ounces	57 g
5 ounces	142 g
10 ounces	284 g
15 ounces	425 g
16 ounces (1 pound)	455 g
1.5pounds	680 g
2pounds	907 g

Appendix 2 Recipes Index

A

Air Fried Salmon Fillets 35
Air Fryer Bacon Wrapped Hot Dogs 51
Air Fryer Spiced Duck Legs 39
Almond Crusted Chicken 42
Apple Crumble 58
Aromatic Cinnamon Lamb Meatballs 52

B

Baked Lamb Steaks 54
Baked Turkey Breast 38
BBQ Honey Pork Ribs 50
Beer-Marinated Duck Breast 39
Best Churros 61
Butter Brownies 61
Butter Oats Cookies 60
Buttery Bagel Crusted Chicken Strips 43
Buttery Chicken Breast 41
Buttery Fried Salmon Fillets 31

C

Cajun Flank Steak 53
Cheese & Spinach Stuffed Chicken Breasts 48
Cheese Jalapeño Poppers with Spring Onion 20
Cheese Prawn Salad with Cherry Tomatoes 28
Cheese-Crusted Tuna Patties with Parsley 29
Cheesy Garlic Broccoli 24
Cherry Crumble 63
Chili Butternut Squash Cubes 24
Chili-Garlic Lamb Loin Chops 52
Chocolate Chip Mug Cakes 63
Chocolate Pistachios Muffins 62
Cinnamon Banana Bread with Walnuts 9
Classic Egg in a Hole 8
Classic Soft Pretzels 15
Crispy Breaded Avocado Fries 19
Crispy Breaded Mozzarella Sticks 15
Crispy Cajun Cod Fillets 34
Crispy Cheese Chicken Tenderloins 38
Crispy Chicken Tenders 40
Crispy Herbed Chicken 43
Crispy Lemony Calamari Rings 14
Crispy Paprika Chicken Legs 46
Crispy Salmon Cakes with Mayonnaise 30
Crispy Spicy Pumpkin Fries 13
Crunchy Breaded Chicken Breasts 37
Crunchy Breaded Chicken Cutlets 40
Crunchy Onion Rings 17
Cumin Cauliflower Poppers 18

D

Delicious Bacon Wrapped Pork Tenderloin 56
Delicious Cheese Beef Taquitos 16
Delicious Cod Cakes with Coriander 31

E

Easy Air Fried Lamb Steak 49
Easy Baked Bagels 9
Easy Baked Turkey Breast 48
Easy Beef Sirloin Roast 57
Easy Butter Cake 58
Easy Potato Fries 19

F

Fresh Crispy Fried Okra 16
Fresh Garlic Butter Prawns with Parsley 34
Fried Apples with Cinnamon Oats 10

G

Garlicky Cumin Chicken Thighs 37
Garlicky Fried Salmon Fillets 29
Garlicky Teriyaki Wild Salmon 28
Gingered Chicken Drumsticks 46

H

Healthy Black Beans & Veggie Burgers 26
Healthy Fried Salmon with Asparagus 33
Herbed Beef Roast with Onion 54
Herbed Garlic Lamb Chops 53
Herbed Garlic Pork Chops 51
Herbed Spicy Whole Chicken 45
Herbs Baked Pork Chops 55
Homemade BBQ Baby Back Ribs 55
Homemade Breaded Tilapia Fillets 33
Homemade Potato Waffle Fries 17
Homemade Sesame Yogurt Bagels 12
Honey & Mustard Chicken Drumsticks 47
Honey Glazed Carrots with Thyme 27
Hot and Spicy Chicken Breasts 44

L

Lemon Cheesecake 59
Lemon-Chili Salmon 35
Lemony Cheese Chicken Breast 44
Lemony Herbed Salmon with Asparagus 36
Lemony Salmon Quiche 11
Lime Mousse 62

N

Nutritious Honey Glazed Tuna Steaks 30

P

Parmesan Asparagus 21
Parmesan Chicken Breasts 47

Q

Quick Balsamic Asparagus 22
Quick Hard Boiled Eggs 8

R

Raisins & Walnuts Semolina Cake 59
Refreshing Balsamic Brussel Sprouts 23
Rosemary Cheese Turkey Croquettes 14
Rosemary Garlic Lamb Chops 57

S

Salty Fresh Kale Chips 18
Salty Garlicky Mushrooms 23
Savoury Fried Rice with Peas & Carrots 25
Simple Air Fried New York Strip Steak 50
Simple Potato Chips 13
Simple Taco Seasoned Lamb Chops 56
Sour & Spicy Chicken Legs 45
Spicy Chicken Wings 41
Spicy Crispy Green Tomatoes 22
Spicy Spiced Butter Courgettes 25
Sticky Tofu in Ginger Orange Sauce 26
Sweet and Spicy Salmon with Sesame 32
Sweet Buttery Squash slices 21
Sweet French Toasts 12
Sweet Potato Chips-Crusted Chicken 42

T

Tasty Beef Roast 49
Tasty Lemony Salmon Fillets 32
Tasty Sweet & Sour Salmon 36
Traditional Avocado Egg Cups 11
Traditional Hasselback Potatoes 27

V

Vanilla Butter Toast 10
Vanilla Chocolate Cake 60